Wow! I discovered something new in Dave Meurer's latest book. Not only is the guy fall-down-on-the-floor, spray-milk-out-of-your-mouth funny (he's been called the Christian Dave Barry), but in *Good Spousekeeping*—the only marriage book I plan to keep on my book shelf from here on out—he's also quite profound and wise. Move over, Dr. Phil, "Dr. Dave" is the new relationship guru in our house.

—*Laura Jensen Walker,*
author of This Old Dump *and*
Dated Jekyll, Married Hyde

How does he do it? Dave Meurer is a genius when it comes to creating a giggle-painted masterpiece. His outrageous wit is insanely compelling, and his insight into marriage is unparalleled among humor writers.

—*Ellie Kay*
author of A Woman's Guide to Family Finances

Good Spousekeeping is very funny and insightful: A good combination! Husbands and wives will enjoy reading this one together!

—*Timothy R. Holler,*
Associate Professor of Psychology,
Crichton College

Dave's work is laugh-out-loud funny and his spiritual insight, cloaked with humor, will help you see God's truth in a new light.

—*Brian Hedrick,*
Editor, Stand Firm

With *Good Spousekeeping*, Dave Meurer cements his reputation as the Christian community's equivalent of Dave Barry. I'm pretty bitter about that—now I need a new career goal.

Good Spousekeeping probably won't actually help men understand their wives (he's funny and insightful, but he's not a miracle worker). Still, guys can have a great time reading it, and their wives will know that at least they're trying. Really, that's about all women can expect.

—Doug Trouten
Assistant Professor of
Journalism at Northwestern College

Seeing Dave Meurer's name on a new book jacket is a red-flag warning for belly laughs and some poignant looks in a literary mirror. Dave's insightful humor is a priceless gift. Every book of his is a delight. This one tops the list.

—T. Davis Bunn, author of
The Quilt, Drummer in the Dark, Innocent Libertine

*The His 'n' Hers
Guide to Couplehood*

Good Spousekeeping

Dave Meurer

LIFE JOURNEY®

Bringing the Message Home for Life

COOK COMMUNICATIONS MINISTRIES
Colorado Springs, Colorado • Paris, Ontario
KINGSWAY COMMUNICATIONS LTD
Eastbourne, England

Life Journey® is an imprint of
Cook Communications Ministries, Colorado Springs, CO 80918
Cook Communications, Paris, Ontario
Kingsway Communications Ltd, Eastbourne, England

GOOD SPOUSEKEEPING
© 2004 by DAVE MEURER

First printing, 2004
Printed in the United States of America
2 3 4 5 6 Printing/Year 08 07 06 05 04

Library of Congress Cataloging-in-Publication Data

Meurer, Dave, 1958-
    Good spousekeeping / Dave Meurer.
        p. cm.
    ISBN: 0-7814-4134-X (pbk.)
    1. Marriage--Humor. 2. Marriage--Religious aspects. I. Title.
PN6231.M3M48 2004
248.8'44'0207--dc22

                                            200407432

To Dale,
the wife of my youth,
who still blesses me after all these years,
I will always love you.

Contents

Foreword

Warning: You are about to laugh harder than you have ever laughed while reading a book. If your recliner has a seat belt, may I suggest that you buckle it, because you're going to fall out of your chair.

But before you delve into this little gem, let me offer another word of caution. My friend Dave Meurer wrote this book not to get cheap laughs or to take potshots at marriage, which is a sacred institution. He wrote it in response to a culture that has made traditional marriage look about as appealing as a boiling cup of hot cocoa on a sunny afternoon … in Florida … in July.

One of Satan's highest priorities is to destroy the covenant of marriage, and too many of us are giving in to the pressure.

We all know the statistics: Basically, half of all marriages now end in divorce. If you think that the church is doing better than the rest of the world, think again. One respected researcher reported that born-again Christians are more likely to go through a marital split than are non-Christians. Scary, isn't it?

The late Edwin Louis Cole, who was married to his wife for fifty-four years, called divorce one of the biggest "plagues" to hit the modern-day church. Even among Christian leadership today there is a crisis of near-epic proportions when it comes to divorce.

Noted author Jack Hayford said that "comfort, convenience and human counsel replace commitment, constancy and the place of the cross in the marriage."

I know, I know … Marriage isn't easy. But is anything worthwhile really easy?

I love my wife more today than I ever have. I admire her on so many levels and for so many reasons. Still, there's one thing

I've learned: No matter how committed you are to one another, conflict is inevitable. Don't tell me it isn't, because it just is!

At its core, marriage is about two imperfect people coming together with a promise to face together whatever problems come along and to stick together for the rest of our lives. When we do, we learn to be less selfish, to focus on the needs of others instead of ourselves-that's a good thing.

Sorry, but there is no ten-step plan that is going to give you a bulletproof marriage—don't buy any book that makes such claims. But there is one thing you can do to make your marriage last. Successful couples have used this "medicine" for thousands of years. That medicine is laughter.

As editor of America's leading magazine for Christian men, and as a happily married man, I realize that most of us guys don't know what makes our wives tick. We want them to react in a certain way. We don't understand why they don't do things the way our mothers did. (Admit it, you really do!)

Truth is, our wives are precious individuals created by God to fill in the gaps where we come up short as men. If we can learn to approach marriage lightheartedly, to stop focusing on the negative, and to choose to appreciate and admire our wives for their uniqueness, we give them one of the greatest gifts we can offer—our acceptance.

In the battle for traditional marriage, one of the church's deadliest weapon comes in a stout, 180-pound package by the name of Dave Meurer. Why? Because he teaches us to laugh at ourselves. More importantly, he helps us to appreciate and treasure our differences rather than to despise them.

Thanks for writing this book, Dave. You're not just tickling our funny bones, you're changing the world.

Robert Andrescik
Editor, *New Man* magazine

Acknowledgments

Producing a book is the closest I will ever come to childbirth. The process contained much toil, sweating, and labored breathing. At the end of the ordeal, when I was bug-eyed and exhausted and yelling incoherently, out popped a baby manuscript that was promptly whisked away for a checkup by the attendant editors.

All authors want their editors to praise their new babies. "My, what a hideous child you have emitted!" is not what we wish to hear. We fear those words because we already got a really close-up look at our offspring, and, deep down, we are saying, "That's not a baby. That's an armadillo!"

Writers are a neurotic group of souls, and we need lots of tender loving care, affirmation, and, occasionally, medication. It is therefore with much gratitude that I thank my editors, Mary McNeil, Dan Benson, and Terry Whalin, who did not cringe at my progeny but loved it.

I also thank my former editor, who is now my agent, Steve Laube. He is the one who first persuaded a publishing house to take a risk on me. He is still wanted in several states.

Saving the best for last, I thank my wife, Dale, for all her support as I worked to complete this project. Dale has been gracious, patient, and always helpful. She still maintains that her childbirth experience was tougher than mine, but I address that misconception in my chapter about living in denial. After all, the insurance company reimbursed her for all her delivery expenses, whereas I had to purchase two reams of paper and several ink cartridges out of my own budget. I know the meaning of suffering.

Reader Warning!

On the American Psychological Association's Standardized Maturity Index, where people like Colin Powell and Queen Elizabeth score one hundred (very mature), the author's score bottoms out at five (ludicrously immature), which places him nominally above the average preschooler but slightly below Daffy Duck.

To alarm you further, be advised that the author is also a congressional aide. This may help explain why many federal policies appear to be huge, sophomoric pranks.

In short, don't expect this to be a deep, serious advice book about marriage. Rather, this is a lighthearted look at "couple-hood" by a quirky guy who has learned that laughter is not only good for the soul but helps out the heart, spleen, and several other internal organs as well. As an added bonus, the author has discovered that his wife has a much harder time staying mad at him (even if he deserves it) if he can get her to start giggling.

All kinds of studies prove that humor is therapeutic. Laughter is a gift from God, and He intends it for our good. Couples need to laugh more—at themselves and at the frustrations of life—so this book is intended to provide a well-deserved dose of merriment. But buried in all the fun stuff are some important, serious themes about commitment, loyalty, understanding, and love. At the end of the book are some "going-deeper" discussion questions based on each chapter. The author hopes these questions will spark some discussion and perhaps even some great romantic sessions. (The author is, after all, a guy.)

He Said, She Said

CHAPTER ONE

WHAT SHE SAID: "Honey, the garden shop is having a big sale today! We can finally plant grass in all those ugly, bare areas next to the fence!"

WHAT HE HEARD: "The court hereby sentences you to a weekend of hard labor."

WHAT HE SAID: "Wow! Benson's Marine is having a blowout sale on bass boats! Imagine us out on the lake, seeing the sun rise and reeling in a trophy fish!"

WHAT SHE HEARD: "Wow, we could hurl thousands of dollars right down the toilet! We can be freezing cold *and* rip out fish guts!"

• • •

Clearly there are subtle differences in the ways that men and women interpret the same information. But why?

After decades of research, scientists have recently concluded that, due to a bunch of complex stuff involving X and Y chromosomes, men and women have totally different genders. (The full details of the federally funded study were published in the June 2003 edition of a medical journal called *Duh*.)

Men and women often react so differently to the same thing simply because God made us differently. He deliberately gave us different biological features and emotional makeups, different strengths and weaknesses, and completely different opinions about craft stores. He further complicated things by giving women the "slow fuse of sexual desire" while granting men the "roaring, forest-fire inferno of desire."

Frankly, I think our world would be much more easygoing and harmonious if women were more like … well, me. They would need to be cuter, of course, but basically like me. I mean, I get along great with myself. No changes or accommodations would be required.

That, apparently, is exactly what God was seeking to avoid. He wants each of us to change, accommodate, and sacrifice for that maddeningly, wonderfully different creature we have chosen to live with, for better or for worse, in sickness and in health, for richer or for spending gobs of loot at the garden shop.

Even when men are at their very best, they are incomplete. Adam is "Exhibit A." He was the perfect human, fresh from the hand of God, but the Creator nevertheless said, "It is not good for the man to be alone" (Genesis 2:18). And so He gave the man a woman. Not just any woman, but a gorgeous *naked* woman! I can almost guarantee that Adam was thinking, *Wow! We should have a romantic interlude this very instant.* And I bet Eve was thinking, *Look at this great garden! We could plant some roses right over there.*

Adam had to learn to understand and accommodate this utterly fantastic, utterly mysterious creature who was so very unlike him and who was yet so necessary to his own sense of completeness. Men have been trying to do the same thing ever since.

I admit that early married life with my wife, Dale, was a difficult adjustment. It wasn't that we didn't love each other; it was that we didn't understand each other. For instance, I did not realize the simple, statistical fact that women use, on average, at least twice as many words per day as men do. And she did not realize that when she asked me what I was thinking and I sometimes said, "Nothing," I wasn't hiding something or avoiding something. It really is possible for me to zone out and think about absolutely nothing. She also had to learn that if I *was* thinking about something, it was often about sex!

After more than two decades of being married to Dale, I am a very different man than I was before I took those scary wedding vows. I am still flawed, but less so. I can look back and see that many of the characteristics God values—love, gentleness, patience, sacrifice—have been developed and deepened within me as a direct result of living day-by-day with the very different creature who is my wife. So, I've concluded that male/female differences are often difficult, but they are inherently good.

And, after all our years together, Dale still finds gardening with me to be highly romantic. She doesn't have quite the same reaction to fish guts, but I figure she just needs more time.

A One-Ring Circus

The day finally came when I couldn't take it anymore. I couldn't keep pretending that everything was fine. So I quietly removed my wedding ring and hid it in my sock drawer. I hoped Dale would not notice but feared it would just be a matter of time.

It took three days.

"Dave, you haven't been wearing your ring lately," Dale said hesitantly. "Is this what I think it is?"

I cringed and stammered, "Well, um …"

"Oh, honey, not again," she said. "We've been through this twice."

"This will be the last time," I said.

"You said that last time," she replied softly.

I knew she was right, but I started desperately grasping at straws. "I think my ring shrank," I said.

Dale's eyes narrowed. "Gold does not shrink. You've already had the ring resized twice, and the jeweler said he can't keep making it bigger."

"Maybe I could get a new ring?" I said hopefully.

"Or how about if we go on a diet for our New Year's resolution? We both could lose some weight."

Panic rose in my chest as visions of cottage cheese and dry toast filled my mind. "Diets don't work for me. Remember how hard I tried last time? It didn't make any difference. All that suffering and torture for nothing!"

Dale folded her arms. "Dave, you only stuck with it for forty-eight hours."

"I felt faint. I got the shakes."

"Chocolate shakes, three of them, at Baskin-Robbins, as I recall," Dale said.

"But—"

"No *buts*," Dale interrupted. "We are going on a diet, and we are going to exercise."

One of the irritating things about spouses is that they often care more about our well-being than we do. It is because of Dale, and *only* because of Dale, that I eat spinach, get prostate exams, and invite complete strangers over to dinner. And I am a better person because of it. "She speaks with wisdom, and faithful instruction is on her tongue" (Proverbs 31:26).

The Gift That Keeps on Taking

CHAPTER THREE

As a change of pace from our typical, predictable Valentine's Day dinner at a restaurant, I really splurged on my wife several years ago and spent extravagantly on a single, memorable, never-to-be-repeated night at the hospital.

Dale slipped into an alluring, one-size-fits-all patient gown featuring the fashionable "open-to-the-air" backside designed by the medical accounting department to ensure that patients cannot flee the building once they see the bill. I even bought her the most expensive bowl of Jell-O on the menu.

Call us romantic. Call us zany. Call us expecting a baby any minute.

For several hours, the room had been filled with puffing, sweating, and sharp cries of pain. And that was just me filling out the insurance forms. Although labor was no cakewalk for Dale, at least she didn't have to try to figure out if our "group number" was the same as our "enrollment code." I certainly did my share of suffering.

Besides, sometimes Dale got downright snippy as her

contractions increased in severity. "If you aren't going to finish your Jell-O, can I have it?" I asked innocently.

"AAAAAAAAAAAARRRRRGH!" Dale replied.

I took that as a "yes."

Dale eventually gave birth to Bradley Michael Meurer, one of the five "Valentine's Day babies" born at St. Elizabeth's Hospital that year. Brad was wonderful. He was adorable. And as I discovered as soon as we brought him home, he was also severely lacking in the personal hygiene department. It wasn't merely that he indiscriminately relieved himself whenever he felt like it; he seemed to deliberately wait until I had his diaper off and was reaching for a new one before he cut loose with a surprise he had been saving just for me.

"Dale, he did it again!" I complained one day. "He is doing this on purpose!"

"Dave, he is one week old. He doesn't do anything on purpose except nurse," Dale replied.

I remain unconvinced. But whether Brad's actions were purposeful or merely coincidental, I figured, *Oh, well. Once we get through this phase, it will be easier.* After all, we had already survived "diaper doom" with our first baby, Mark.

The problem was that by the time we got through "hygienic-lapse" phase, we were well into the "I-want-to-go-to-the-Toys-R-MINE!" stage. Greed and selfishness are big agenda items for preschoolers. So Dale and I dealt with issues like sharing, taking turns, and not picking your nose or the nose of anyone else. Before we knew it, both of our kids were into the junior-high-school, "I-need-extremely-expensive-tennis-shoes" phase.

Do you see a trend here? Every single phase has some new and difficult challenge, so by the time parents sort of get a handle on one phase, we've transitioned into another one that is at least as difficult, and in many cases *more* difficult, than the phase we've just survived! Dale and I have spent our entire parenting career wondering when things will get easier, and it hasn't happened yet!

The Bible reveals that "children are a gift [from] the Lord" (Psalm 127:3 NASB), and they truly are—but they are an extremely high-maintenance gift. My expanded version of the Bible renders Psalm 127:3 this way: "Children [uncivilized heathens who need to be not only converted but also bathed regularly and force-fed their vegetables] are a gift [nonreturnable and nonrefundable even if you kept all your hospital receipts] [from] the Lord [the sovereign and compassionate Lord of the universe who puts up with *way* more from you than you will ever put up with from *your* children]."

Parenting is taxing, exhausting, difficult, and maddening. It is also wonderful, fulfilling, important, and a divine call. But even in the *best* of circumstances, parenting is hard. Accept that fact and keep plugging away at it. If your kids are young, let me encourage you by pointing out that no matter how difficult a time you are having now, things will get worse when the raging teenage hormones kick in. As they say in the French army, "I feel so much better now that I've given up hope."

Good Spousekeeping

CHAPTER FOUR

One of the special joys of being a writer is getting hostile, enraged mail from spittle-spewing critics who just can't believe that any decent publisher would print my kind of worthless, shallow drivel. (I keep asking my mom to stop writing to my publisher, but she has an independent streak wider than the state of Montana.)

I have no doubt that the title of this book will generate yet another batch of incensed mail from somewhat-less-than-adoring readers. In fact, I can pretty much write the basic letter for them:

Dear Male-Chauvinist-Swine Author of the So-Called "Book" Titled *Good Spousekeeping*:

We *hate* your new book, which implies that a spouse is to be "kept" by her domineering, possessive male partner. It is repressive, belching, idiot cave-men like *you* who are perpetuating the patriarchal, condescending, oppressive culture that enlightened persons have been working to improve.

Plus, the thinly veiled reference to a magazine that deals with domestic, historically female duties sends a message that women should be chained to the hearth while they slave over your nonvegetarian dinner. We haven't read the book, because the title says it all, you fathead.

> Sincerely,
> The Entire Faculty of the
> Women's Issues Department
>   The University of Sensitivity, New York

So perhaps I'd better pause to explain what I mean by "good spousekeeping."

First, note that the title of this book does not indicate that only one gender is "keeping" the other. That ambiguity was deliberate because the title is intended to include both husband and wife. I simply mean to convey that both partners are called by God to be "good" to each other and to "keep" their vows, thereby "keeping" their marriage. *Good Spousekeeping* is fundamentally about encouraging husbands and wives to understand each other better, work together, and protect their marriages—and laugh more. Also, I needed a clever title, and the good ones like *Gone with the Wind* and *Jaws* were already taken.

Over many years of putting my written words into the public arena, I have learned that what really bugs some people is not, fundamentally, my ideas or how I state them. What really bugs them is the foundation on which I build my words. For example, if the Women's Issues Department rejects marriage as a man-made social construct that has been foisted upon powerless women, then any book affirming that God gave the good and wholesome gift of marriage to humanity is not going to pass muster with these critics.

I would be the last one to argue that marriage has not been abused through the centuries. Indeed, in some cultures marriage is little more than slavery. But biblical marriage, as outlined in the New Testament, can hardly be called oppressive, mean, or degrading. I mean, the God-given order to husbands is to "love your wives, just as Christ loved the church and gave himself up for her" (Ephesians 5:25). That is a standard of truly staggering proportions. Jesus always did what was in the best interest of the church. He served, gave, and loved to the point of death. True, the church is called to "submit" to Jesus—there's that word!—but why in our right minds would we not want to trust the wisdom and leadership of a God who is so wholly and completely committed to us? If we clearly see the model upon which the institution of marriage is based—the God who is passionately in love with his people and who takes great joy in our reciprocating love—we will gain an entirely new perspective on what marriage can and should be.

A big part of what I call "good spousekeeping" not only includes improving our relationships with our spouses but also encompasses helping each other better understand the God who not only invented marriage but who is the very definition of love. In a mysterious way that we can't fully understand or explain, there is a third person present in a Christian marriage. "Christ in you" is how the Bible puts it (Colossians 1:27).

As we live out healthy, loving, kind, giving, and sacrificial relationships with our spouses, we are not simply being good marriage partners. We are tasting the love of God. We are catching snippets of heaven. We are teaching each other deep lessons about the Author of love. God wants each of us to experience the best that earthly love has to offer and then realize that His own love for us far exceeds the richest love our spouses can possibly bestow upon us. This is very cool. God is waaaaaay better, kinder, and more passionate toward you than you have ever hoped or imagined Him to be.

However, when any marriage becomes twisted, perverted, or broken, it becomes wholly different than what God intended or commanded it to be. It ceases to perform its God-given purpose. It grieves the heart of God. But we shouldn't chuck the idea of marriage simply because some people have mucked it up any more than we should swear off food simply because some people have used it to pursue gluttony.

Our God-given call to marriage is the call to care for each other, to serve each other, and to honor each other—in short, to love each other. It is a call for us to always do what is in the best interest of our beloveds. It is a call for each of us to help our partners be the very best they can be.

How can the critics argue with that?

Happy Feet

CHAPTER FIVE

One year, as a special Mother's Day surprise, I took Dale to see a troupe of Irish style dancers, all of whom had a severe case of Celtic Hyperactive Foot Syndrome. You cannot imagine how fast those people pranced and tapped for two hours. I couldn't have moved my feet that briskly if I were walking on hot coals or getting an IRS audit.

"Weren't they amazing?" Dale asked after the performance. "Don't they make you wish you had become a dancer?"

"Well, their skills are not terribly practical," I replied. "I mean, those are the last people you would pick to clear a minefield."

Um, not that I felt clumsy in comparison.

To be perfectly honest, I have often felt a pang of embarrassment about the many skills I lack. I am a lousy athlete. When I go swimming, tanned young people routinely try to rescue me. And, unlike my dad, who would never dream of actually paying someone else to replace the brakes on his

Chevy, my version of "working on the car" consists of changing the wiper blades.

My three brothers are all skilled with their hands. When my older brother wanted to add a room to his house, he did it himself. One of my younger brothers is an accomplished automobile painter and custom painted his vintage car. If I tried to add a room to my house or paint my car, the final result would look like the work of vandals.

One day I confessed to one of my brothers that I felt awkward when I compared my abilities with his. "Are you kidding?" he asked, looking stunned. "You can *write*! We're all amazed at *you*."

None of us can do it all. God has given each of us various gifts and abilities that are uniquely ours. This is true in both the physical and spiritual realms. We all benefit from the rich blend of our many gifts and talents. We need the doctors *and* the artists, the mechanics *and* the soldiers, the pastors *and* the plumbers. The key is to find your niche, both in your occupation and in your spiritual life, and to use your gifts and talents well to the glory of God.

Dale does a lot of things well that do not come easy to me. Hospitality is part of her nature, and she has a history of inviting strangers over for dinner. Some of our lifelong friendships would never have been launched had Dale not taken the initiative to strike up a conversation with a new person or couple who walked into church looking a little lost or overwhelmed.

I am glad that Dale has strengths in areas where I am weak and vice versa. We are a better couple because of the different mixes of abilities and interests we bring to our marriage. And you know what? Even though I will never be an accomplished dancer, I take heart from the realization that probably none of those dancers can write a decent memo.

Look What You Signed Up For!

CHAPTER SIX

A leading child-development specialist recently reached an alarming conclusion: The average developing fetus, at about 6,100 days after conception, mutates into a sixteen-year-old kid. Dr. Samuel Finster, who made this shocking discovery, issued an urgent warning to prospective parents:

> Most couples get pregnant with the hope of bringing a healthy, happy baby home from the hospital, thereby enriching their lives. But in the overwhelming number of cases we have tracked, the sweet and adorable babies eventually transform into moody, adult-sized, carbon-based life forms who will deplete your life savings just to purchase acne medications. The males can strip your refrigerator bare in nanoseconds, and the females will spend so much time in front of the mirror that you may need to install major appliances in the bathroom. We were also horrified to

discover that these dangerous organisms can legally drive in most states.

If Dr. Finster sounds a little testy, it is because his son recently turned sixteen and was driving alone for the first time in Dr. Finster's car—a Volvo—while eating a cheeseburger and fries. When a poodle scampered in front of him, fortunately the brakes worked exceptionally well, but the CD player is completely full of strawberry milk shake residue that will *never* come out.

There is a very good reason why God arranged for our children to start out so cute and innocent and fun. If He had inflicted a teenager on Adam and Eve, they immediately would have ceased having more children, and the average college textbook on the history of civilization would be a *lot* shorter. You see, God had to ease us into parenthood by cleverly disguising potential teenagers as gurgling little babies who disarm us by cooing and smiling before they barf on us.

If the average couple could see just how difficult parenting teens is going to be, they would run screaming down the road. But since God emphatically wanted children in the world, He not only made them cute, He also made the process of conceiving them so much fun that He knew we would participate in His plan.

Make no mistake, married persons, God is manipulating you. It is no accident that sex is so enormously pleasurable that you *completely forget* you may eventually get a teenager out of the deal. God uses sex to temporarily lower our IQs, thereby ensuring that we will bring children into the world. And these children typically become teens.

Teenagers are inherently difficult. They are often maddening, immature, unreasonable, and capable of stupendous acts of stupidity—which is to say that they are exactly like you and I used to be when we were teenagers. Yet God loves them deeply, and He wants you to help them through this very difficult phase of growing up. Your teenagers need massive amounts of your time and energy, even if they act like they don't want anyone to know they even have parents.

What they mostly need is a relationship with you, not a rule book. I am not saying that rules are unimportant. Indeed, they are vital and potentially even lifesaving. In our family, Dale and I have regularly invoked rules, curfews, and commandments despite the caterwauling of protest. Rules come with the territory of being parents. But rules minus a relationship will likely spawn rebellion. That is where many moms and dads go wrong.

We parents need to show grace to our teenagers, just like God shows grace to us. Grace is about love. It is about sacrifice. It is about relationship. It is not about "laying down the law." It is about laying down our lives. God did it for His children, and He wants us to do likewise for ours.

If our teens are driving us insane—and they all eventually do—we need to keep reminding ourselves that the main thing they need to know is that we love them. Even if we discover that they have been doing disturbing things behind our backs. Even if we need to take away the car keys. Even if we are so hurt we could cry, or so mad we could just spit— they need to know we love them.

Even when God told Adam and Eve that they had to leave the garden because of their willful sin and open rebellion, He never ceased loving them. If anything is going to bring a wayward teen back, it won't be a spittle-spewing fit of rage on your part. It will be love.

Jesus did not come to earth to shout at us. He came to win

us back through sacrificial love. Hang in there if times are tough. God has been in your shoes. He knows what you are going through, and He promises to walk with you.

A Moving Experience

CHAPTER SEVEN

When it comes to summer family fun, there is nothing like the adventure of packing up all your belongings and shoveling them into a U-Haul with a nonfunctioning air conditioner, to make you wish you had scheduled a kidney transplant instead.

I could not believe the wads of assorted objects, knick-knacks, gadgets, and Tupperware that flowed like a mighty river from our house into the groaning orange-and-white Ford parked in our driveway. As I staggered out the door carrying yet another box of domestic tranquility, I wished I had more rigorously observed the biblical command to avoid storing up treasures on earth (Matthew 6:19). But on reflection, I realized that there was very little treasure involved, unless a complete collection of Robot Ninja Mutated Penguins counts as "treasure."

We weren't moving bars of gold. We were just moving the stuff of our lives: a lamp I bought for Dale at a quaint store on the coast, an old-but-comfortable wing-backed chair, and several cubic yards of photographs.

Moving was mostly my wife's idea. Anything that involves picking up furniture and putting it somewhere else is always her idea, whether we are talking about moving the couch across the room or across town. Unlike Dale, I am a creature of habit. I resist change (in the same sense that a geologic formation is a creature of habit and resists change).

Years earlier when Dale wanted to redo the nursery, I objected and pointed out that it looked fine the way it was. "Do you remember how long it took to get the Noah's Ark wallpaper up?" I complained. "And now you just want to tear it down?"

"Dave, the boys are both in high school now!" she said.

"Yes, but if we leave the room alone it will be perfect when we have grandchildren," I replied.

She was not persuaded. I think she was just too proud to admit the logic of my point.

But back to our summer move. After facing yet another stack of boxes, the boys staged a mini-revolt. "There's too much junk!" Brad exclaimed. "Can't we throw some of this stuff away?"

"Yeah," Mark agreed. "Let's just toss a bunch of it in the trash!"

"I really have weeded a lot of it out," Dale replied defensively, "but I guess we could always toss out some old things we don't use."

"Good," the boys replied simultaneously.

Dale picked up a deck of dog-eared "Old Maid" cards and tossed them into the trash.

"*What are you doing?*" Brad cried, lunging for those cards as if they were the crown jewels of Spain.

"What's wrong?" Dale asked, clearly surprised.

"Don't throw away the stuff we grew up with!" Brad said. "We loved to play this game!"

"Yeah!" Mark chimed in. "Have you no sense of sentimental value?"

Instead of lightening the load, we actually ended up packing buckets full of *rocks* removed from the flower beds because we had gathered many of the stones over the course of several years from all sorts of places we had visited during family vacations. Given sufficient time and a big enough jackhammer, I think the kids would have loaded up the driveway solely because they had used it for years as a makeshift basketball court.

Ultimately, all the objects we moved on that sweaty summer day are destined to perish. None of the stuff will follow us to heaven. That's one of the reasons God tells us to take the long view and to avoid hoarding that which the world deems "treasure." But I believe that the good memories we collect as a family are riches we get to keep forever. The sacrifices we make for each other, the good deeds we do, the love we share—these treasures will last.

Middle Ground

I sat on the edge of my seat, scanning the sky and waiting for the massive twin-rotor helicopter to come into view. I couldn't wait to see the chopper drop a car several hundred feet smack into the sun-baked, rock-hard dirt. It would be the highlight of the air show—a tire-popping, metal-crushing, glass-smashing spectacle of high-energy destruction.

"I don't get it," said Dale.

"Hon, it's just *cool*! There's nothing to *get*! It's just the rush of watching it happen! Maybe there will even be a ball of flame!"

"But I still don't get it," she said.

This is the same woman who dragged me into a hoity-toity San Francisco art gallery and made me look at bizarre paintings by some guy whose "art" features what appear to be melting clocks. "I don't get it," I had said.

"Well, look at his intent. Look at what he is saying about time. You need to stand here and really study it," Dale replied.

So I stood there and tried to really grasp it. It was an agonizing ten seconds. "I still don't get it," I said.

The gallery salesperson gave me the "you-filthy-cretin" look, so I moved to another part of the building and found myself in a sculpture display featuring California's most impressive collection of Hideous Wads of Metal priced as much as a new Winnebago.

A salesperson glided up to me. "Powerful, isn't it?" she said.

"Indeed," I mused. "I think the artist was trying to capture the angst of an Oldsmobile sedan that realizes it has been dropped by the helicopter of judgment onto the unforgiving tarmac of mortality."

She edged away from me.

The only art object I purchased that day was a T-shirt that read "Member of the Official Alcatraz Swim Team."

Dale will never relate to my love of Tom Clancy novels, and I will never understand how she can read *Anne of Green Gables* without slipping into a coma. When we were first married, we tried to do almost everything together. That lasted about a month. I could easily spend an entire day gawking at a vintage car collection, while Dale could only last about thirty minutes before she began to twitch.

"Isn't this a great '57 Chevy Bel Air?" I would gasp in awe.

"It looks just like the last three dozen we looked at," she would respond, frowning.

When Dale took me with her when she shopped for shoes, I would literally slip into advanced dementia, shuffling slowly through the aisles and drooling.

It didn't take us long to learn to focus on areas of overlapping interest, as demonstrated in the following diagram:

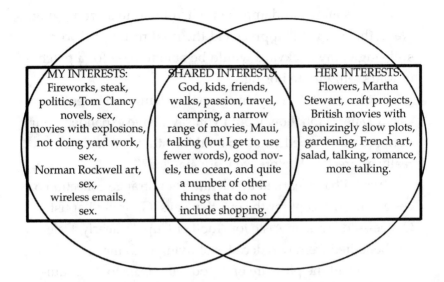

MY INTERESTS: Fireworks, steak, politics, Tom Clancy novels, sex, movies with explosions, not doing yard work, sex, Norman Rockwell art, sex, wireless emails, sex.

SHARED INTERESTS: God, kids, friends, walks, passion, travel, camping, a narrow range of movies, Maui, talking (but I get to use fewer words), good novels, the ocean, and quite a number of other things that do not include shopping.

HER INTERESTS: Flowers, Martha Stewart, craft projects, British movies with agonizingly slow plots, gardening, French art, salad, talking, romance, more talking.

We have different interests not only because of our personalities and backgrounds, but because God hardwired men and women differently. But even though we have our distinct areas of interest, one of the secrets to growing together is to keep expanding the circle of shared interests.

Dale learned long ago that I would rather ditch a plane into shark-infested waters than to ever enter another fabric store as long as I live, and I have given up any hope that she will ever enjoy my favorite spy novel. But there are other areas where we have both budged.

Because Dale is such an avid lover of plants, flowers, and all things beautiful, I have developed a real appreciation for the way a backyard can be transformed into a place of peaceful beauty by means of carefully selected foliage. Indeed, what she did to the yard of our last home was incredible. I didn't mind sitting on the deck and sipping iced tea, watching her toil and dig and lug shrubs around in a wheelbarrow. (That lasted all of five minutes, and my bliss was somewhat dampened when I had to start digging. Nevertheless, I still appreciated the final result.) If I were still single, my backyard would be able to pass for a patch of Mars, only more boring.

But I am not the only one who has changed. I recently asked Dale, "Hon, how would you say I have expanded your horizons and helped you admire things that you had not really appreciated before we were married?"

"Well, I have learned to tolerate your strange collection of coffee mugs, except for the one that says 'Gourmet Baptist Coffee—I'd Walk an Aisle for Another Cup.'" Clearly, Dale has benefited from two decades of living with me.

I also had the pleasure of introducing Dale to the exquisite music of Bach and Handel. She grew up on "pop" music and had no experience with the rich world of classical music. So we would take trips to the coast, listening to the angelic voice of a soaring soprano until her sublime song was rudely interrupted by the *click-thunk* of my eight-track cassette changing tracks. (If you are not old enough to know what an eight-track tape is, I bitterly resent your youthfulness. For the record, eight-track cassettes were crude audio recordings chiseled from solid granite by primitive, cave-dwelling employees of the Maxell Corporation.)

In addition to expanding each other's appreciation of new things, Dale and I have truly expanded each other's appreciation of God. One of the biggest "aha!" lessons of my life occurred when I realized that Dale knew me better than anyone else on the planet, and that even with all my faults and flaws and stupidity, she loved me deeply. And it occurred to me that since she could not possibly love me more than God, His love was waaaaaay deeper, higher, and broader than I had ever dreamed possible.

All forms of love are pale imitations of that deepest and richest love—the love God has for us. I believe that this is one of the biggest truths God wanted me to learn, and He taught it to me through marriage. Dale and I still have our own circles of interest, but the best of these is the shared circle.

It's What's Inside That Counts

CHAPTER NINE

As any award-winning pastry chef can tell you, the key to creating a visually enticing Angel Food Spam Cake is to carefully conceal all the little chunks of salty reconstituted meat product deep inside the cake and then cover everything with whipped cream. That way, unsuspecting guests have no idea about the pending assault on their taste buds until it is too late.

I invented the Angel Food Spam Cake in 1986. I toiled and toiled over the recipe until I got it just right. It goes like this (feel free to copy it for your own recipe box):

1. Buy a cheap, unfrosted angel food cake at the grocery store.
2. Buy a can of Spam.
3. Hide chunks of Spam in the cake.
4. Frost the cake.
5. Serve to unsuspecting people.

If *Good Housekeeping* ever sponsors a contest titled "Truly Dreadful Desserts to Foist on Clueless Guests," I am a shoo-in for first place.

For reasons that Dale will never quite understand, one year I decided to bring an Angel Food Spam Cake to a workplace Christmas party. "It will be fun," I told her.

"It's weird and disgusting," she replied.

"That's what's fun!" I said.

(Unlike many women who appreciate husbands who help with the cooking, my wife gets very territorial and kind of twitchy when she sees me pull out the flour, sugar, pickles, sardines, chocolate chips, and celery. Although Dale is a great cook in her own right, she knows *nothing* about adding a little excitement to a church potluck.)

So I took my cake to the annual Christmas party and set it on the table. The assistant manager, Jerry, was the first one to venture close to the bait.

"I made it myself," I said.

"Wow! Looks great! I think I'll try it," he replied.

"Let me cut it for you," I offered, grabbing the knife and sawing off a generous slab of a dessert that contained roughly as much salt as Lot's wife after her mishap.

I worked hard not to stare as Jerry took a big bite. Although his reaction took only about three-quarters of a second, let me break it down for you in a series of slow-frame shots, kind of like what NASA does when it produces a film showing a slow-motion rocket launch. When one is savoring a moment, one does not want to rush it, does one?

Jerry's mouth paused in mid-chew.

A vague look of alarm creased his brow.

Then his eyes bulged.

His nostrils flared.

His corpuscles constricted.

His face flushed red, then went white.

His tongue telegraphed an urgent message to his brain: "S-P-I-T T-H-A-T O-U-T N-O-W!"

His feet spun for traction, much like the tires on a dragster, as he lunged for a wastebasket, where he hurriedly ejected my culinary creation.

"There's something salty and squishy in your cake!" he snarled.

"Spam," I replied.

"You put Spam in a cake?" he roared.

Regrettably, he made such a scene that everyone else was forewarned. On the plus side, I hadn't technically violated any store policies, and thus he couldn't fire me. (He checked.)

Well, I can hear you thinking, *this is an odd story for Dave to tell at this point. What possible connection does this have to building a good marriage?* I'm glad you asked!

The point is that life is full of enticing, eye-pleasing delights that have been carefully frosted to hide the truly disgusting stuff inside. Many a marriage has been wounded, sometimes mortally, when one or both partners are enticed by something that is unhealthy/bad/dangerous, but looks really good on the outside.

(Pause for a moment while I get into my serious, theological mode.)

I believe in the existence of a personal, intelligent, evil force who goes by the name of Lucifer. Living in opposition to God, he tries to get back at God by messing up the objects of God's love—us. I believe the devil makes a concerted effort to destroy marriages as part of a broader scheme to take down entire societies and nations. And his chief tool is deception.

Let's use materialism and greed as one example. One thing Jesus told us is that we should "store up ... treasures in heaven" (Matthew 6:20) and not be greedy or materialistic. Objects are not the fundamental source of joy. In a hundred different ways, the Bible reveals that we will find joy as we love God and love other people. In fact, Jesus said, "it is more blessed to give than to receive" (Acts 20:35). (Generosity is a great antidote to materialism.) The apostle Paul flatly calls greed "idolatry" (see Colossians 3:5). Yet countless advertisements reinforce the message that bliss will come in the form of a product that is sleekly packaged in a thirty-second commercial.

All too many couples get on that treadmill and start an exhausting run to nowhere. So many of them seem to focus inordinate amounts of time and energy on the acquisition of stuff. They believe that their aching void—the yearning for happiness—will be filled by a bigger house, a better car, or a more elaborate vacation. In short, they believe it will be filled by storing up treasures on earth. The accumulation of stuff—and massive debt—can keep couples working long and hard to pay the bills, and the relationship can suffer from neglect.

I am not an ascetic. Dale and I do not live an austere and severe lifestyle. But we recognize that materialism is a temptation to be avoided, not a goal to pursue. So we live in a manner that we think is reasonable, which includes budgeting money to give away in support of God's purposes.

When I went to the bank to qualify for a mortgage, the loan officer offered to lend me a huge amount of money. She was trying to be helpful, but she might just as well have cheerfully said, "I'll help you become a slave to your debts! I can bring new levels of stress into your home!" We took out a much smaller loan for a much smaller house. And it is perfect for us.

God focuses on our relationships—with Him and with others. We need to give the gift of time to each other. How many people do you know who have "made it" financially but whose marriages are in the tank? There are corporate executives who would pay virtually any amount to have better relationships with their children, but you *can't* pay to have a better relationship with your kids! It takes *you*. It takes time.

I am not talking as much about income levels as I am trying to emphasize an attitude of the heart. I know wealthy people who have their heads on right. They are loving God, loving their spouses, loving their kids, and serving in many ways. They are not materialists, even though they are rich. And I know a guy who has almost nothing and has ruined all his relationships but who is *obsessed* with getting rich. The orientation of the heart is the key.

Satan's implicit promise in all temptations—materialism, pornography, affairs, alcohol and substance abuse—can be summed up like this: "This will make you happy. This will fulfill you. This will take away your pain." But Satan always lies. He often makes good on a short-term thrill, but he thinks long-term. Too often, we don't.

My Angel Food Spam Cake analogy breaks down at this point, because when poor Jerry took a bite out of it, he was innocent and had no clue. He had not been warned. But God warns us, emphatically. Imagine walking past Satan's bakery and holding God's hand as He explains, "See that apple dumpling on that shelf? It looks good, doesn't it?"

"Yes, God, it does," you reply.

"Well, the devil has added extra ingredients just for you," God says.

"Like what?"

"Like rancid squirrel guts he scraped off the road."

"That's disgusting!" you reply.

"Yes, it is," says God. "Plus, he added some rattlesnake venom and three tablespoons of Drano."

"That's awful!"

Imagine God talking you through each outwardly tempting

dessert and explaining what's really inside it and how it will hurt you if you eat it. Then He takes you to His own bakery, which is full of good and wonderful and fulfilling foods, and says you can pick whatever you like. Then He lets go of your hand so you can choose.

Sooner or later, we all end up with our noses against the window of Satan's bakery while he whispers that God is a killjoy. "What does He know, anyway?" he croons. "Would you like to try a glazed doughnut?"

Yes, that doughnut looks really, really good. And we vaguely recall God warning us about this, but our stomachs are growling and our mouths are watering, and it can't be all that bad, can it? Something that looks this good? Maybe just one bite, just to see …

A Sight for Sore Eyes

CHAPTER TEN

I had never been a believer in UFOs or aliens until I had one of those uncanny experiences you read about in supermarket tabloids. I vividly remember the eerie event, even though it happened a decade ago. I was walking through our house when a blur of motion outside the front window caught my eye. Two smallish, humanoid-shaped blobs stood on our grass, and floating back and forth between them was a saucer-shaped object. I froze for a moment, then called for Dale.

"Try not to make any sudden moves," I said softly as she came into the room.

"What's wrong?" she asked, alarmed.

"I don't want to scare you, but there are two alien life forms on our front lawn. They look vaguely human, but their features are indistinguishable. Something is floating between them, possibly a communication device or even a weapon."

Dale peered out the window, then slowly turned back and faced me. "Vaguely human?" she asked. "Dave, those 'alien life forms' happen to be our children, who are playing Frisbee. You need glasses."

She made an appointment with an eye doctor and insisted on driving me there.

"Read the top row of letters on the chart," said the optometrist.

"Um, I think that first one might be an *M*, but it also kind of looks like an *S*. Or a *B*. Is it a *Y*?"

"You need glasses," he said.

"Doc, I'm worried," I replied. "Is it normal to have this kind of sudden, dramatic loss of vision?"

"It wasn't sudden," he stated. "Your vision has been deteriorating slowly over time—it happens to most of us—and you just got used to seeing poorly. It took someone else to bring it to your attention."

Often the "someone else" is my spouse. In addition to my poor vision, I have all kinds of blind spots. I sometimes don't notice myself being harsh and critical. I don't see how I walk over other people's emotions. My perspective can be so skewed that I don't perceive just how badly I have misjudged a person or situation.

Dale has helped me on more than one occasion when I failed to discern the difference between one of our sons having a bad attitude and him needing to talk about something that was troubling him. She has continued to pray faithfully for people and for marriages that I had quietly written off as lost causes—and they came back from the brink. She has helped me to see inside myself and explore a deeper problem that I chalked up to "having a bad day." Sometimes I don't even know what's bugging me. For a lot of guys, anger masks a different problem. Our spouses can often be more objective than we are, so it's important for us to listen attentively.

I buy my glasses from the optometrist, but when I really need to have my vision sharpened, nothing beats having Dale look me square in the eye and say, "I think you need to take another look." She can see me in ways I can't. And I am the better for it.

Raiders of the Posh Park

CHAPTER ELEVEN

Dale's ideal way to spend a Saturday morning is to engage in a form of urban warfare she calls "yard sale-ing." Preparations for this operation rival anything ever planned in the Logistics Division of the Pentagon. On the night before each Operation Get-a-Good-Deal, Dale pores over the classified ads and maps out a strategy to rapidly hit all key targets during pre-dawn raids.

When Dale is joined by a team of similarly disciplined female comrades (specifically, her sister-in-law Beth), they constitute an unbeatable squad of battle-hardened, professional bargain hunters. They can spot an underpriced wicker table in the back of a garage faster than a UN weapons inspector could find a Scud missile in his own bathroom.

For years, I tried to avoid accompanying Dale to yard sales. My ideal version of what constitutes a successful Saturday morning differs somewhat from hers, in the same sense that Custer's view of a successful Battle of Little Big Horn differed somewhat from the Indians'. On any given

Saturday, I like to lie in bed, possumlike, until 10:00 AM. I am not a morning person, and it often takes a team of paramedics thirty minutes to inject a sufficient dose of French Roast java directly into my veins before they can detect a pulse.

But one day, Dale asked me to come with her on a particularly vital mission. "It's the annual neighborhood-wide sale in a very upscale area," she explained. "These people will dispose of expensive, practically new furniture because they decided the color does not match their new cat. I may need help loading things into the van. You'll have fun! Honest!"

I seriously doubted I would have fun, but I wanted to be a good husband and show an interest in my wife's hobby. Little sacrifices like this make for a good marriage, and the Bible says men should be willing to lay down their lives for their wives. Although getting up at 6:00 AM on a Saturday to go pawing through wads of used stuff is not exactly death, it is awfully close. So I gulped down my coffee, and we climbed aboard a troop carrier that had been cleverly camouflaged to look like our Chrysler minivan.

We soon found ourselves in occupied territory called Uppington Park, or something like that, cruising slowly past driveways crammed with what appeared to be the entire contents of the local mall. I sauntered over to a rack of wire shelves that were identical to the shelves I had purchased days earlier for seventy bucks. The little sticker read $3.00. I blinked. "Dale!" I hissed.

She came over.

"Does that sticker say what it seems to say?" I asked.

"Yes," she replied.

"You mean I could buy this for three bucks, take back the one I didn't open yet, and save $67.00?"

"Plus tax," she replied.

I bought the wire rack, a patio umbrella, a computer desk, and a slew of other bargains. "Hurry!" I urged Dale. "There are people down the street looking at things I could potentially buy! They could be getting *our stuff!*"

The morning was going so great that I was wondering how it could get any better when I spied something that freeze-dried my liver. Could it be a ... Why, yes, it was—unbelievably—the yard-sale equivalent of the crown jewels of England, over in a corner, largely obscured by other yard-sale debris.

I casually draped my body over the coveted treasure and asked the homeowner, "How much?"

"Five bucks, and there are two more just like it in the shed if you want them," she replied.

I tried to look calm, but my hands were shaking as I forked over the money. I stashed the valuables in the van, then wandered over to my wife. "I got the deal of the century," I whispered to Dale.

"What?"

"I can't say it out loud, or we might get robbed," I said. "I'll show you when we get to the car."

Once we were safely away from prying eyes, I unveiled the trio of rare collectibles. *"Voilá!"* I said, throwing off the protective blanket. "Three 1970s-vintage United States Air Force bomb casings with almost no rust! Look at the fins on these things!"

Dale stared, speechless.

"Amazing find, huh?" I said.

"What on earth are you planning to do with them?" she asked.

"Well, for starters, I'll slap a glass top on one of them and use it as an outdoor table and conversation piece. The next one I will use as a seasonal decoration in the front yard, probably painted red and green and adorned with festive twinkling lights. The last one I'll turn into a birdbath for the front lawn."

Dale forbade me to buy anything else for the duration of the day. I suspect that she felt embarrassed by my superior ability to sniff out a yard-sale bargain.

As we moved from yard to yard, I finally noticed that Dale was scooping up gobs of clothing that would fit a young girl. Since both of our children are boys who are of voting age, Dale's purchases raised a glaring question. "Um, is there something I need to know?" I asked.

"How does this look?" Dale replied, holding up a little outfit with angels embroidered on it.

"I don't think it will fit you," I said.

"It isn't for me!" she replied.

"Well, I don't think the boys will wear it, and I know I won't, so why are we buying little-girl clothes?"

"For Mandy,"* Dale replied.

A light clicked on, and I suddenly understood that "yard sale-ing" for her is far more than a mere hobby—it's a ministry.

Mandy is a sweet little girl from a very poor family. Dale had talked about her and prayed for her many times. Mandy attends the school where Dale works in a program targeted at children who struggle with the basics of reading and writing. Some of these kids have inherent learning disabilities, but many live in the chaos of evictions, constant moves, incarcerated parents, and ever-changing "significant others" who move in and out of their lives. Some of these kids have never been read to before they arrive at school. Dale and her bargain-hunting friends tactfully and discreetly help out kids whose families have very limited resources.

"Hon, that is really sweet of you," I said. "But how do you pull it off? There must be some kind of permission process, some kind of legal mumbo jumbo that governs whether you can do this."

Dale explained that when school staff or parent volunteers notice a child without a coat, for example, they contact the parent or guardian and ask if it would be okay if the "Parent Club" provides some basic clothing or personal-care items. Local retailers will donate some clothing, but Dale and her like-minded allies carry things one step further and shop for specific sizes and styles to help out some of the more needy kids. Mandy held a special place in Dale's heart. Later, when Dale presented Mandy with her "almost-new" outfits, the little girl exclaimed, "They're perfect!"

In Proverbs 31:10, 20, King Lemuel asks, "A wife of noble character who can find? She is worth far more than rubies. ... She opens her arms to the poor and extends her hands to the needy." I think my wife is a "Proverbs thirty-wonderful" woman.

As an added bonus, Dale said I never have to go to another garage sale again. In fact, she has forbidden me to come. She says I need my sleep. Is she thoughtful, or what?

*Name changed.

The Stockings Weren't Hung by the Chimney with Care

CHAPTER TWELVE

Although the Christmas holidays are fraught with numerous opportunities to blow the family budget, I am pleased to report that last December Dale and I managed to hold our unbudgeted yuletide spending to slightly less than a quarter million dollars. Thankfully, insurance covered most of it.

Our teenage son, Brad, had been feeling lousy the week leading up to Christmas. The doctor diagnosed his problem as the flu and prescribed the "lots-of-fluids-and-plenty-of-rest" routine. But after several days, Brad became worse instead of better.

We went back to the doctor, who ordered a series of blood tests that revealed a white blood cell count that was higher than normal. I say "higher than normal" in the same sense that I'd say a forty-five-story house is "higher than normal." A typical white cell count is between 5,000 and 7,000. Brad's was a stratospheric 30,000.

An MRI revealed Brad's abscessing appendix. Our son was being slowly, quietly poisoned. So we hospitalized him, signed a dozen forms we didn't read, and sat nervously in a waiting room while two doctors performed an evening surgery. An appendectomy can be fairly routine if the condition is caught early enough, but Brad's case was considerably more complicated. The infection and fever had sapped so much fluid from his system that nurses pumped nine liters of liquid into Brad's body in two hours. *Nine liters.*

Several hours after the surgery, he went into shock. The next forty-eight hours were a blur of medical activity, tears, prayers, and quick naps on waiting-room furniture. We spent Christmas in the intensive care unit as a medical team worked to save Brad. His heart was pounding at the machine-gun rate of 190 beats per minute, and he was hooked up to no fewer than a dozen wires and tubes.

It was not the kind of Christmas depicted in the Hallmark commercials. There were no gifts, no songs, no stockings hung by the chimney with care. And none of that mattered. All we wanted was Brad.

After Christmas, he was heavily sedated and asleep most of the time, but a few days after the surgery he opened his eyes and whispered, "Ask them how long it will be until I can go snowboarding again."

Leave it to a teenage boy. We had half the city praying for his survival, and he wanted a snow report.

His physicians kept him on a two-week regimen of powerful antibiotics, trying to beat the wicked infection that kept his white cell count hovering at 20,000. Eventually, the surgeon reluctantly decided to open Brad back up to look for hidden pockets of infection. "I hate to go back in, but antibiotics are not resolving it," he said. "Unless I see a dramatic overnight drop in his white cell count, I don't have any choice."

Everyone prayed.

There was a dramatic overnight drop in Brad's white cell count. The surgeon grinned at us the next day and said, "Well, you folks have been praying for a miracle. Maybe you just got one."

Within a few weeks, Brad was back on the slopes.

Looking back at last year's Christmas season, I would characterize it in two sentences:

1. It was awful.

2. It was the best Christmas ever.

These sentences pretty much summarize the first Christmas, too. So much went wrong for Mary and Joseph: a long and difficult trip during the end stages of pregnancy, no room in the inn, ending up in a smelly stable to give birth. But in the middle of so much that seemed so wrong, God was there to work out His will. That truth was, and continues to be, a great gift.

Stretched to the Limit

CHAPTER THIRTEEN

As part of my wife's ongoing effort to expand my horizons, she periodically insists that I eat a completely unnatural food item, such as cauliflower. I think my horizons are perfectly fine just where they are, bolted safely to the concrete. Cauliflower was clearly not intended to be consumed by humans, which is proven by the fact that it does not appear on the menu list at McDonald's. Ditto for kiwi.

"If it has hair on the outside, it is not a fruit" is one of my long-standing dining mottoes. But Dale thinks I am too narrow in my tastes, from food to art, so she believes part of her marital mission is to broaden my perspective.

Thus we recently found ourselves right smack in the middle of San Francisco's ethnic sector, sitting in a tiny restaurant in which virtually no employees spoke English. Before we ordered, Dale turned to a nearby couple finishing their dinner and asked if they had enjoyed their menu choice.

"It was marvelous," answered the woman.

"What did you have?" Dale asked.

"I have no idea," she said. "We just let the waiter pick something for us. Just ask him for whatever we had. You'll love it."

"How exciting!" Dale said, thanking the woman as she left.

"Exciting? How about *insane*?" I whispered.

"It will be an adventure," Dale replied.

"You have got to be kidding," I stated. "I have seen enough *National Geographic* documentaries to know that there are places in the world where people think it is the height of culinary joy to eat a bird that has been buried for six weeks. For all we know, those satisfied customers just ate a rancid penguin."

Dale got that junior-high-school-teacher look in her eyes. "Dave, we *are* going to try something different," she stated.

"*You* can have something dangerous if you want to, but the most exotic thing I'll try is a sweet-and-sour Big Mac," I whispered.

Being in her adventurous mode, Dale simply told the waiter to surprise us before I could protest. I hoped he understood her.

"You go first," I said to Dale when the waiter brought the first course.

She tasted it and grinned. "Whatever it is, it is really wonderful."

I tried a small particle on the tip of my fork.

"Well?" she asked.

"Hmmmm, it is pretty good," I replied. "But I feel an overpowering urge to put on a tuxedo and slide down a snowdrift."

To be perfectly honest, each course was incredibly good.

Even the thinly sliced yams in prune sauce were great. I finally had to admit that to Dale.

Next time I go to McDonald's, I think I'll see if they can put prune sauce on my Big Mac. And maybe I'll even think about what Paul wrote to the Corinthians: "Eat whatever is put before you without raising questions" (1 Corinthians 10:27).

Passing on the Past

One of the most helpful pieces of marriage advice I have ever heard is this simple maxim: "Don't live in the past."

For instance, one day Dale unfairly dredged up the fact that I once borrowed her vehicle and returned it with .00675 ounces of gasoline vapor in the tank. "It was so frustrating to see the needle below the *E* after you took that trip out of town," she said.

"Dale, Dale, Dale. Don't live in the past," I said empathetically.

"The past? What are you talking about? I went out this morning and the van was empty," she replied, frowning.

"Exactly," I said. "This morning is part of the past. We need to just move beyond the past. A marriage expert said so in a book."

Dale folded her arms and said, "How convenient. According to that argument, I should never discuss any inconsiderate thing you do because, technically, it happened in the 'past.'"

"Exactly!" I replied, delighted that she grasped the logic of my point.

"Dave, if you want to have a *future* that lasts more than five minutes," she retorted, "don't tell me again to not live in the 'past' when you're talking about something that happened several hours ago."

I almost mentioned that she needed to work on her "anger issues," but she was getting that twitching problem with her left eye so I decided not to risk it. There is nothing quite so volatile as a woman with anger issues who keeps living in the past.

Another useful phrase that will immeasurably help your nuptial relationship is this handy line: "Hon, I think you are in denial." This line is particularly handy when you need to rapidly change the subject.

For example, let's say that a husband is driving by an auto dealership and stops in just to look around. One thing kind of leads to another and, after all, the old rig *was* looking a little worse for the wear. So he makes an executive decision to buy a new car.

WIFE: "You traded in your work truck for a brand-new Thunderbird convertible? Have you utterly lost your mind? The car is completely impractical and we can't afford it."

HUSBAND: "Hon, I think you are in denial."

WIFE: "*Me?* You think I'm the one in denial? You are the one who just made a $48,000.00 impulse purchase, and you are accusing *me* of being in denial? *Denial about what?*"

HUSBAND: "Your anger issues."

The real danger in responding this way is that a jury of her peers would probably agree with her. And if the jury were comprised of mostly women, they would probably not only convict you but also whack you with their purses as they filed out of the jury box.

But there is one final phrase that covers many bases, and it seems to work remarkably well no matter how many times it is tried. That powerful phrase is, "I'm sorry. Will you please forgive me?"

The trick to employing this phrase successfully is that it can't be a trick. You need to really be sorry, and you need to prove it by changing your offensive behavior. Your spouse's forgiveness will be tied directly to the sincerity of your apology, which has to be backed up by positive and sincere actions.

Saying "I'm sorry" without changing your behavior is *really* living in denial.

Happily Maui-ed

On our twenty-second wedding anniversary, Dale and I found ourselves at a five-star hotel on the romantic island of Maui, where we watched a spectacular sunset, lounged at the pool, and dined on hot dogs.

I was wearing a fashionable T-shirt that had the words "Unathletic Department" emblazoned across my chest, and Dale was wearing an emergency backup shirt she had bought at a tourist shop for $9.99.

We did not have a room at that hotel. Rather, we had pool lounge chairs, which we attempted to sleep on until the rain started. No one asked us to pose for a photo for *Romantic Getaways* magazine.

Let me explain.

We had already wrapped up our weeklong vacation earlier that day, but our flight back home to California was canceled due to the Great East Coast Power Fiasco of 2003. If you are wondering why a flight from a *Pacific* island to the

West Coast was impacted by a power outage on the *East* Coast, I can sum it up for you in two words: *charter flight*.

In an effort to be thrifty, we had booked very affordable seats on a small airline that, to avoid any legal problems, I will refer to as "Fred's Frugal Flites" (company motto: "Pray That Nothing Goes Wrong"). When the power went out in New York, where Fred's Frugal Flites has its headquarters (in Fred's garage), the pilot was unable to communicate with Fred Central. So he could not file a flight plan as required by the Federal Aviation Administration (motto: "We don't *care* whether the pilot has flown that route 500 times and could do it blindfolded; we want a flight plan").

Planes were leaving Maui right and left, but only because the major airlines have advanced communications devices such as cell phones. I think Fred is too frugal to own a cell phone. I suspect he is too frugal for all kinds of "extras," such as fax machines and indoor plumbing. But for whatever reason, the airline's crew could not communicate with Fred Central.

So, the flight that was supposed to leave at 2:30 PM did not. All 214 of us stranded, thrifty passengers milled around the airport for a few hours, occupying ourselves with useful tasks such as rearranging the receipts in our wallets, until a nervous spokesperson informed us that the plane could not take off because the flight crew had exceeded the minimum "rest period" required by the Federal Department of Mandatory Rest Periods (motto: "Naps are good for you. We learned this in kindergarten. Please get us a graham cracker and milk when we wake up.").

"But we are going to bus you to a five-star hotel and feed you dinner!" exclaimed the spokesperson.

I turned to Dale and said, "Hon, if we have to be stranded

somewhere on our anniversary, we might as well be stranded at a luxury hotel on a beautiful Hawaiian island."

The spokesperson motioned for attention and continued: "Um, you can't actually stay at the hotel because all the rooms are booked. But you can hang out by the pool until midnight, when we will put you back on the bus and return you to the airport for our return flight, which we now believe will leave at 3:00 AM. Our technicians are busy right now making arrangements to retrieve the flight plan from the carrier pigeon Fred is training. We are having the hotel set up a buffet for you, and we suggest that you pile on as much food as you can because Fred is only springing for one trip through the line. Oh, and we have all your luggage sealed in the plane, so try not to spill anything on yourselves. If you need to freshen up, just kind of sneak into one of the lobby restrooms. Did you know that you can take a 'paper-towel bath' with just six paper towels?"

Dale and I looked at each other. "Happy anniversary," I said.

"You, too," she replied.

"Let's make the best of it," I said.

Dale smiled. "Hey, we *are* still in Maui!"

That is how we found ourselves having hot dogs on our big day. To be fair to Fred, that isn't all that we were offered. There were also burgers. And one pass through the soda machine. (Fred was certainly not going to go overboard.)

But Dale and I made the most of things—taking a long walk on the beach, visiting some shops, and buying a few more mementos. Sure, the flight delay was inconvenient, but we reminded each other that we were hardly suffering. The colonists suffered. The pioneers suffered. The Chicago Bears fans suffered. We were merely delayed. So we had pretty good attitudes. In fact, I was feeling downright spiritually mature.

When we were finally schlepped back to the airport, we learned that the crew had still not been able to reach Fred Central, so we would not be taking off at 3:00 AM. We were to sleep on the airport floor or contort our bodies to fit the airport benches which had wicked twists and curves that appeared to be specifically designed to make sleep either agonizing or impossible. (I think they were created in the Middle Ages by professional torturers.)

INQUISITOR: "Dost the infidel still refuseth to recant? We hast ways of makingest thou changest thy mind!"

PRISONER: "I beg thee! Not the whip!"

INQUISITOR: "Ha, ha, ha! Thou wishest! We are stickingeth thee on the Maui airport seats of doom!"

PRISONER: "Nay! Anything but the seats of doom!"

INQUISITOR: "Pluseth, we are bookingeth thee on Fred's Frugal Flites!"

PRISONER: "Can I just have the whip instead?"

At 5:00 AM, I phoned a real airline and learned that two one-way tickets home would cost us the equivalent of the gross domestic product of Brazil. I declined.

At 6:00 AM, I was not feeling nearly as spiritually mature as I had felt hours earlier when I was strolling on the beach.

At 7:00 AM, I staggered up to the Fred's Flites' spokesperson and said, "Let's just suppose that, for whatever reason, you discover that you will *never* reach Fred Central. At what point do you start putting us on the flights of other airlines?"

"Sir," she answered, "we have been trying all night to see how many of you we could put on other flights, but with most flights already booked and with more than 200 of you, it could take—"

"Days," I said, finishing her sentence.

She winced, bracing for me to be as hostile and nasty as several other passengers had already been to her.

"Well, I know you are doing what you can. It isn't your fault," I said.

She smiled. "Thank you."

Eventually, using an emergency communication system that involved two empty tomato-sauce cans and 6,000 miles of string, Fred Central was able to communicate with the crew. We took off at 9:00 AM. The return flight featured the same movie we had seen during the arrival flight. Fred apparently bought the movie and intended to get his money's worth out of it, but everyone was so wiped out that it didn't matter.

Twelve hours later, we staggered into our house, threw our luggage on the floor, and flopped into bed. We slept for fourteen hours. I snored.

On the romance scale, the evening did not register a "ten." But we were alive, we were well, we were home, and we had each other. And we will never forget the week of really great days we had on Maui—snorkeling, swimming with a sea turtle, and taking a sunset sailboat ride.

In a sense, our Maui trip was a microcosm of our entire human existence. It was a mixed bag of good and bad, joys and frustrations, highs and lows. We can't choose whether or not we will experience frustrations in life. We can, however, choose which attitudes we will bring to bear during these times. And our attitudes have far more to do with our happiness than what Fred's Frugal Flites feeds us for dinner.

"Don't Give Me Any More Lip!"

CHAPTER SIXTEEN

Two men outfitted in dark suits, dark glasses, and small hearing devices moved purposefully through the crowd, informing people that it was time to sit down—now! The man who was the Main Event would not enter until everyone was seated.

The location was the convention room of a downtown hotel, and the occasion was a political fund-raising event. The per-plate cost was about twenty times what each guest would have been charged for the identical meal at the same hotel on an average night. But this was not an average night. The elevated lectern at the front of the room was graced with the circular Great Seal of the United States.

I was not a paying guest. I was there because my boss, a congressman, was also in the crowd of people waiting for the Main Event to walk on stage to the cue of trumpets blaring.

I am an aide. On this particular evening, nothing seemed to remotely require any of my typical aide-like functions, but my boss had graciously invited Dale and me to attend anyway. (Dale was helping to staff the ticket table. It was another thinly veiled reason to get us both in the door for what promised to be an incredibly memorable evening.)

"I still can't believe this is about to happen," Dale said, straightening my tie in a nearby room.

"Any minute," I replied.

A deep, resonant voice came over the loudspeakers. "Ladies and gentlemen, the President of the United States!"

The crowd gasped and rose to its feet as the majestic strains of "Hail to the Chief" filled the room. Two men in suits flung open the doors, and heads began bobbing and weaving as all eyes strained to catch the first glimpse of ... me.

I waved in what I hoped was a presidential manner and shook hands as I made my way toward the stage. My gray wig was about two sizes too small, but it was all the costume shop had available. I looked like a very, very poor imitation of President Clinton, but I tried to compensate by exclaiming, "Shazam!" to each person who shook my hand.

My boss, who had not been informed that I would provide the evening's entertainment, burst into great, gasping guffaws of mirth and had to sit down before he collapsed.

I ascended to the lectern, the music faded, and I motioned for quiet. I had been practicing my "State of Confusion" address for weeks. I planned to call for several new spending initiatives, beginning with a proposal to address the chronic crisis of infants who are born without teeth. Citing decades of research that proved virtually all infants are born toothless, I would call on Congress to fund my bold "Free Dentures for All Babies" initiative to solve this unaddressed emergency.

Almost as important as the content of my address was the delivery. I had practiced several of Bill Clinton's more pronounced facial expressions, including his trademark "stick-out-lower-lip-while-looking-thoughtful" pose. I used that expression several times during my speech, and it generated laughter and a few groans. All in all, the evening was a success—except for one small, unanticipated problem.

A few days later, while I was sitting at the dining room table mulling over a stack of bills, Dale asked, "Just what are you doing?"

"Well," I said, "I'm trying to figure out whether to just pay off this Visa bill or stretch it over a couple of months," I said.

"I'm not talking about the bills. I mean, what are you doing with your lower lip?"

"Nothing," I replied, puzzled.

"Dave, you were doing that Bill Clinton lip thing!" she exclaimed.

"I was? *Shazam!* I didn't know it!"

In the following weeks, Dale spotted me umpteen times adopting that dratted pose. And I was truly unaware that I was doing it.

To make matters worse, whenever something surprised or alarmed me, I exhibited other echoes of Clinton. If I spilled some coffee or bumped my knee, for example, that event was often followed by, "Shazam!"

My skit took place in 1998, but much to Dale's chagrin I still unconsciously slip into "lip mode" on a regular basis, so she has committed herself to eradicating these bad habits from me. "Hey! Lip!" she will scold from across the room, prompting me to retract my lip faster than a lizard recoils his tongue.

It is amazing how easily a bad habit can move right in and make itself at home. I wish my Clinton-lip was my only bad habit, but I have more. For instance, I never intended to become overweight. I mean, as a small child it was not my dream to one day look suspiciously like Danny DeVito's twin. But when I left a fairly active job (stocking shelves and walking around all day in a grocery store) and settled into a fairly sedentary desk job (where the most active thing I do involves using a letter opener), basic laws of biology began to take over. If you research the bodies of Olympic athletes, you will discover that none of them got that way by typing memos.

One of the great things Dale does for me is help me change the course of my life. It is because of her that I have begun taking long walks (she comes with me). It is because of her that I at least have a bottle of vitamins in the cabinet, and I am working to develop the habit of taking them. It is because of her that fresh vegetables are a part of my diet. It is because of Dale that I will someday get this lower-lip thing under control—but possibly only after she employs a behavior-modification technique involving duct tape.

In addition to helping us get rid of bad habits, our spouses can help us recapture good habits. There was a time in my life when, for several reasons that are too complex to get into here, I dropped what had been a consistent habit of reading my Bible. I also dropped church. And prayer. And just about anything that had to do with God.

I was hurt, angry, and confused about a situation in which I felt God had really let me down. So I withdrew. I didn't launch into a life of reckless sin. Indeed, from the outside most people didn't notice anything different about me. But I just kind of slipped into neutral and stopped caring about God or His opinion of anything.

There was no way Dale could have hounded me back to the right path. And she did not try to. Nagging is not one of the fruits of the Spirit, and it typically generates an obstinate heart far more than it brings repentance. But she just kept loving me through a very dark and disappointing part of my life. It was scary for her, and she was pretty much on her own spiritually. But she entered our marriage for better or for worse, and this was one of the "for worse" times. Her love remained constant, for better or for worse. I believe love, more than anything else, is what brought me back around to God.

Sometimes we make the huge mistake of looking at a bad habit—poor behavior in ourselves or in our spouses—as the "thing in itself." We see it as The Problem, although it is really a symptom of a deeper problem. This is not to say the Bad Thing, whatever it is, does not matter or does not need to be addressed. But we need to get at the Big Issue that is usually lurking behind the Bad Habit.

Let's say a spouse develops an unhealthy or dangerous habit—excessive use of diet pills, alcohol, drugs, worka-holism, fill-in-the-blank. It is vital to address not only the bad habit but the issue that gave rise to the habit. Many very bad, destructive, and dangerous habits result when a spouse is trying to escape an overwhelming sense of emotional pain. Nagging about the bad habit may drive the habit under-ground, but it doesn't fix anything. We need to understand what is really going on.

Sometimes the issue is too big for a couple to tackle on their own. That's where the church—the tangible expression of Christ in the world today—can play a powerful, restorative role. This doesn't mean that the couple has to spill their guts to everyone, but it very well may involve spilling their guts to a small core of loving, mature, trustworthy people. This is one of the reasons the Bible cautions us in Hebrews 10:25, "Let us not give up meeting together, as some are in the habit of doing, but let us encourage one another—and all the more as you see the Day approaching."

Habits can be a curse or a blessing, depending on the nature of the habit. During more than two decades, Dale has become a blessed habit. I can't get over her, and I don't intend to try.

No Joke!

CHAPTER SEVENTEEN

The year was 1964, and I intended to pull off a truly exceptional April Fool's Day joke that was so brilliant, so daring, and so convincing that future generations would marvel at it. At the tender age of six, my fertile little brain had masterminded a scheme that required a dedicated team to implement it. My co-conspirators (a hodgepodge of neighbor kids and my brothers) had gathered on the side of my house, safely out of adult view.

"Okay, on the count of three you start screaming, and I'll do the rest," I whispered.

Six little voices began caterwauling in a cacophony of utterly believable dismay. I sprinted as fast as my tiny legs would carry me, leaped onto the porch on the back of our house, and flung open the door. My mom was just pouring another cup of coffee for Mrs. Dietz, our next-door neighbor.

"David, don't slam the—"

"Mrs. Dietz's house is on fire and the kids ran out but the baby is inside!" I interrupted.

The result was far more spectacular than anything I had dared to hope. Mrs. Dietz dropped her coffee mug and emitted an atom-splitting screech that peeled the linoleum right off the floor. My mom became airborne, her legs spinning like eggbeaters as she tried, Flintstones-like, to gain traction on the waxed floor.

Both women broke the Olympic sprinting record as they shot from the house and barreled across the lawn, urged on by the panicked screams of my tiny assistants.

When they got to the property line, we all yelled in unison, "April fool!"

Tragically, neither Mrs. Dietz nor my mother demonstrated any appreciation for the wit and cleverness of our festive April jest. Without going into unnecessarily vivid detail, let me simply note that within a few weeks most of us kids could once again manage to sit down for dinner.

Years later, my still fertile and yet underdeveloped mind was continuing to hatch practical jokes. In high school, I organized the Great Garbanzo Conga Line. I got the entire yearbook staff to march down the street to our teacher's house as we played a conga tune on kazoos. We knocked on her door, and when she opened it we conga-danced through her house, each of us handing her a can of garbanzo beans as we passed by.

I also got in *major* trouble with whoopee cushions. Enough said.

When I was seeking Dale's hand in marriage, I managed to rein in my immaturity just enough to convince her that there was hope for me. But within a few months, I was back at it.

Dale was washing dishes one evening when I drove home from work and saw an opportunity to amuse myself with yet another practical joke. Instead of coming through the door, I crept around the side of the house, mashed my face against the kitchen window, and waited for her to glance up and notice my contorted expression.

It took a minute, and when she finally saw me she screamed. It was not an amused, "Oh-you-got-me" scream. It was raw fear. She could not tell it was me, and from the looks of it, some leering weirdo was trying to break into the house.

I rushed inside, feeling like the biggest idiot in the world (which I was), and found Dale in tears. When she was finally able to talk about it, she was justifiably angry and hurt. It was not a "joke." She pointed out that most men cannot relate to the deep fear women have about being alone and unprotected as a strange man tries to break in. I apologized profusely and never did anything remotely like that again.

Many years later I read a Scripture passage that seems to have been written for me: "Like a madman shooting firebrands or deadly arrows is a man who deceives his neighbor and says, 'I was only joking!'" (Proverbs 26:18–19). I believe that humor is a gift from God, but like all gifts, it can be abused. I learned that the hard way.

Laughter is still a big part of our marriage, and I hope it always will be. But here is a guideline: If only one of you thinks something is funny, it isn't.

What's in a Name?

CHAPTER EIGHTEEN

When I was young, my sister dated a guy who drove a sporty, blue-and-white MG named "Fang." I drooled over that two-seater rocket on wheels and dreamed of someday having a similar car with a similarly cool nickname.

Regrettably, none of my subsequent cars were British convertibles. At one point, I owned an AMC Pacer, which was voted "Ugliest Car of the Year" by a major automotive magazine. The Pacer looked like an enormous metal toad, and it handled with the precision and speed of a diseased buffalo. It was not the kind of car you could even name "Molar," much less "Fang."

I eventually owned a VW Rabbit, and I toyed with naming it "Warrior," but that seemed like a stretch for a vehicle that was named after a furry creature with enormous ears and buck teeth.

Years turned into decades, and none of my modest cars ever seemed eligible for an exotic nickname. However, I recently purchased another car and decided I finally had my big chance to bestow a fitting title on my gleaming automobile. Although it is not exactly a sports car, it is in decent shape considering that it had well over 100,000 miles on it when I bought it.

I enthusiastically pulled Dale and our two sons, Mark and Brad, together to run a couple of names by them. "I've narrowed it down to two options: 'Thunder Lizard' or 'Sea Biscuit,'" I announced.

"That is the lamest thing you have ever said," replied Brad.

"Why can't you act like a normal father?" asked Mark.

"Dave, it is a white Chrysler sedan—a recliner with a steering wheel," Dale commented.

"But 'Fang' was already taken," I pointed out.

Dale got that involuntary twitch in her left eye and stood up to take a nap.

"I'm leaning toward 'Thunder Lizard,'" I said as she staggered from the room. "I know a guy who can paint the name in cursive script on the trunk."

My boys emphatically opposed both names. "*Please* don't do this to us," they pleaded, "*especially* not in front of our friends!" (Unfortunately, Brad and Mark are quite familiar with the biblical command directing fathers to "not exasperate your children" [Ephesians 6:4]. They find it necessary to quote it often.)

In an effort to compromise, I offered to name the car "Thunder Biscuit," but they were not in a negotiating mood. So I won't have the cursive lettering done, and I have even abandoned the idea of painting flames on the front fenders. That is the kind of caring, sensitive, and sacrificial person I am. Plus, Dale made an elaborate show of handing me sheets and a blanket for the couch. I know when I'm beat.

The reality is that, for me, the days of cool cars with cool nicknames are long gone. Indeed, shortly after my sister and her boyfriend got married, "Fang" was replaced by a much more conservative vehicle—a family-friendly car they named "Fangly." That nickname was a wry admission that time changes things. And it should.

Part of growing up—as both a person and a Christian—involves what the Bible calls putting away "childish ways" (1 Corinthians 13:11). All the external, shallow things that we obsessed over during high school should have taken a backseat long ago to the real issues of life.

My car is not my identity; it is transportation. My identity is wrapped up in the astonishing fact that the God of the universe calls me His own. He loves me relentlessly, understands my weaknesses, and forgives my sins.

Besides, in an effort to meet me halfway, Dale agreed that we can nickname the car "T. B." That isn't quite as glamorous as "Thunder Biscuit," but marriage is nothing if not compromise.

I am still working on convincing her to call me by my preferred nickname. I don't want to be known merely as an "author"; I prefer the more noble title of "Awe-Thor," which combines reverent fear ("awe") with the name of the mythical Viking god of thunder ("Thor").

Dale hasn't quite warmed to this nickname yet, but Rome wasn't built in a day. So if I just give her a few hundred years …

An Imperfect Christmas

With candles glowing softly in the living room, snowflakes floating quietly into our front yard, and the Bible opened to that familiar "shepherds abiding" story in the Gospel of Luke, it was a picture-perfect Christmas Eve—until the coffee table erupted in flames.

In keeping with part of my German heritage, our family has always opened at least one present on the night before Christmas. Somehow a piece of wrapping paper got too close to a candle. It did not merely ignite; it exploded. I blew at it, an effort that merely slid the flaming debris off the table and into another pile of paper on the floor.

Instinctively, I began stomping on the paper in an effort to smother the flames. This is an effective way to stop a small fire unless you happen to be wearing brand-new, furry lion's-head slippers, which will immediately flame to life like some kind of mythological beast roused from its thousand-year slumber.

In less time than it takes to sing "presents roasting on an

open fire," our quiet holiday evening was transformed into a modern-day version of Dante's *Inferno*, only stupider and less poetic.

"Grab that thingy!" I yelled to Mark as I performed an impromptu version of "River Dance" (albeit with more smoke).

"The hose?" he yelled back.

"The red thingy that sprays stuff," I barked.

But Dale had already grabbed the fire extinguisher and began blasting away. In a roar of white mist, the flames died out and the room was filled with gently falling ashes.

We all stared quietly at the mess. My lion slippers sported melted whiskers, the coffee table bore scorch marks, and the floor was covered with a white, powdery residue belched from the extinguisher. We opened the doors and windows to clear out the smoke and spent the evening cleaning up. I don't think we ever got back to the shepherds abiding peacefully in their fields. And I finally gave up on my quest for the "perfect" Christmas.

For many years, I had embarked on a futile attempt to achieve that elusive ideal—the romanticized holiday captured in cards, magazines, and thirty-second television commercials. The ingredients seemed so simple: a warm fire glowing in the hearth, hot cider and cinnamon sticks brewing in the kitchen, the warm flicker of candles, the glow of the tree, and my family snuggled together on the sofa as we recounted the touching story of Mary and Joseph and the baby Jesus.

But every year, something went wrong. The hearth belched smoke back into the room, a drink got spilled, the nativity-scene camel got knocked over, or one of the boys asked if he could play a video game right when the angels were about to bring tidings of great joy.

As each year passed without me realizing my dream of a perfect Christmas, I became progressively more uptight, obsessive, and ridiculous. "All I want is one perfect holiday, just one!" I complained to Dale.

"Dave, we have kids! It will *never* be perfect," Dale replied. "But can you just let it be *good*? Can you just enjoy what actually *is*, instead of what you think it *should be*?"

As is so often the case, my wife was right. It was irritating at the time, but she was right nevertheless. The perfect Christmas is a myth. After all, the first Christmas was hardly perfect. It was glorious and difficult, miraculous and earthy, sublime and sweaty, tender and harsh. Angels' songs were mixed with animals' smells. The hopes and fears of all the years were jumbled together as heaven invaded a stable.

Nothing has really changed since then. Christmas is still a mixed bag. Our hopes and fears still meet. There is the joy of the children and the aching loss in the heart of a surviving grandparent who will never again be with her beloved spouse at Christmastime. There is the uncle who will be a boor and the nephew who will be a delight. In the shallow materialism of the marketplace, hymns and carols will be played *ad infinitum* as background shopping music. And yet in the solemnity of the Christmas church service, those hymns and carols will again move us to tears, to joy, to hope.

Christmas may not be perfect. But it can be good.

An Inescapable Conclusion

CHAPTER TWENTY

Paul wrote in Romans that human beings can deduce certain things about the nature of God by studying aspects of His creation, and in that vein I think the study of sex leads us to an inescapable conclusion: God is nice.

God did not *have* to make sex a wonderful and fulfilling experience in order to propagate the human race. Because He is all-powerful, He could have arranged for us to experience an involuntary episode of cellular division. You would be sitting in a business meeting or changing the oil in your Oldsmobile, and you would start to stretch like Gumby and—*presto*—there would be two of you. Or, God could have programmed you to periodically emit a little pinecone that would take root and hatch a new human being. Or God could have made it painful to *not* reproduce, perhaps by making you watch nonstop reruns of *The Partridge Family* until you agreed to have a child.

Instead of doing any of that, God made marital sex an

incredibly enjoyable experience. I think this was very nice of Him.

Of course, I could use a word other than *nice*. I could use a biblical word, such as *kind* or *gracious* or *loving*. All of these adjectives would be true. But I think that we sometimes get inoculated against certain words because we hear them so often. There are many Christians who, regrettably, can say, "God is kind and gracious and loving," while feeling that He is angry, distant, and punishing them. So I will stick to my word choice and reiterate my assertion—sex proves that God is nice.

Sex also proves that He wants us to gasp and pant and sweat and clutch each other and do all those things that we can't help but do while we are making love, even when we are trying to be quiet so the kids won't hear us. God made sex feel so wonderful that it is hard to contain our expressions of happiness. An unkind God would not have dreamed this up; an unkind God would have made sex an experience akin to an IRS audit.

Some of us come into marriage with all kinds of emotional and psychological baggage that makes us feel like sex is bad or dirty. We may have picked up this attitude from the family or culture in which we were raised, we may feel guilty about past sexual activity in which we violated God's commands, or we may have been traumatized by sexual crimes committed against us. But whatever its source, the sense that sex is inherently dirty or unspiritual is based on a flawed view of reality.

Sex is only ugly, dirty, and cheap when it is selfish, shallow, and uncommitted. It is dirty when a guy is on the prowl for a cheap thrill. It is ugly when a man fathers a child and refuses to be a dad. It is deeply sad when a woman allows herself to be used simply to escape loneliness and to pretend that she is loved when she knows she does not have the real thing.

God created us to be intensely sexual creatures, so sex is by definition good. He made us crave sensual touch. But He also gave us firm boundaries, such as the foundational command that we only are to have sex after we make the mother of all commitments in front of God and the assembled witnesses to be with our spouses for better or for worse, come what may. Uncommitted sex is unkind sex. It is sinful. It is sinful because it so deeply violates the very nature of what God intended sex to be. God has reasons for everything He commands. His rules are not arbitrary. They are intended for our good.

In addition to being kind, God is also, well, kind of coercive. I don't know how else to put it. I certainly don't say this critically, but I don't know how else to describe this glaringly obvious plan of God to entice men and women into a lifetime commitment to each other.

He emphatically forbids sexual relations apart from marital commitment, but even that firm commandment reflects His kindness. His intent is to make sure we don't engage in sex simply to use other human beings for our selfish and narrow purposes. God wants sex to be inextricably linked, for each of us, to a sweet oneness with one other soul of the opposite sex. That, too, is nice of Him.

Sometimes marriage does not turn out that way because people do not follow through on their promises. Or a tragedy strikes; this is a fallen world, and bad things happen. But the intent of God is clear. He gives us this powerful attraction toward a special someone, and He tells us to commit ourselves to be faithful and loyal and loving toward that person for life or … to go hungry. He does not want us to cheapen, water down, and/or muck up His plan by taking sex out of the context of a giving, sacrificial, binding marital relationship. This loyalty and love-to-the-end is an inherent part of His kindness. He is loyal and loving and faithful, and He wants us to be like Him.

Sex within marriage is sublime. It weaves a man and woman together—body, soul, and spirit. It makes us happy and contented, and it even burns up extra calories! A mean God would have made sex fattening. God is nice!

Read the Instructions!

CHAPTER TWENTY-ONE

It was not until Dale and I moved for the fourth time that we found ourselves living in a home that had an integrated lawn-watering system. Until then, the most complicated watering system we had encountered consisted of our kids squirting each other with the hose on a hot summer day.

The advantage of the modern lawn-watering system is that it turns itself on and off, it covers the entire lawn, and you can pretty much ignore it until something breaks. The downside is that a little computer runs it, so every time there is a power outage you face the exact problem you face when your VCR is blinking "00:00" for years because you are a middle-aged person who did not grow up with digital equipment and are doomed the split second you have to reprogram anything.

When we moved into our new home, the watering system's computer was blinking. I asked my neighbor for help, and he kindly reset it for me. He also explained how to increase and decrease the time of the watering cycles as the seasons changed. I nodded the entire time he was explaining the details, but what I actually heard sounded like someone speaking Cantonese. Now when summer comes around and the lawn needs more water, I walk into the garage and hit the one button I understand, which reads, "manual on." I press that button, and the system turns on. If we are preparing to go on vacation for a week, I hit the "manual on" button seven times the day before we leave. The yard becomes a swamp, complete with bayou creatures and schools of fish, but I figure it will at least stay damp until we get home.

To be honest, I like the lawn-watering system I grew up with. Uncomplicated and virtually indestructible, it consisted of a hose and a small, round, metal sprinkler that contained no moving parts. I turned on the faucet and water sprayed out of the sprinkler. Although I had to move the hose every twenty minutes—and I often forgot to move it and therefore wasted enough water to irrigate a field of broccoli—it was nevertheless a system I could operate without experiencing severe feelings of inadequacy.

But my new and "improved" lawn sprinklers contain as many moving parts as a Toyota engine, and these parts don't last forever. Last summer, two sprinkler heads quit working effectively within a few days of each other. They would still pop up out of the lawn but would only spray one place.

The clear solution was to go out every day when the water turned on and scamper back and forth between the sprinklers, manually pointing them in different directions. But Dale, demonstrating her tendency to be unreasonable and demanding, asked me to go to the home-improvement store and buy replacement sprinkler heads.

Now, those of you who are mechanically inclined are undoubtedly shaking your heads and muttering, "For crying out loud, Dave, changing a sprinkler head is not exactly rocket science." But bear in mind that I am the guy who was banned for life from my high school woodshop class after the unfortunate incident wherein a two-by-four got fed into the wrong end of the buzz saw, which grabbed the board and hurled it through the wall at 450 miles per hour.

(If you ever see me in the garage, bent over the engine of my car, I am not fixing it. I am praying for it. And I am still hoping that federal investigators don't really find out why the entire East Coast power grid went down, but I will confess that my hand was touching a kitchen appliance when it happened. I fear there is a connection, even though I was several thousand miles away at the time.)

Nevertheless, I went down to the store and bought replacement sprinklers.

I dug up the old ones.

I screwed in the new ones.

I took a deep breath, turned on the water, and watched with satisfaction as water arched forth gracefully. I had actually fixed something without harming myself or anyone else in the process!

It was such a thrilling sight that I contemplated a career change—"Dave's Advanced Water Solutions," with a base rate of $50.00 per hour. I would get my own truck, place a sign on the door, and drive forth in confidence to deliver the masses from their defective lawn-watering systems. Saint Dave, the patron of sprinkler-impaired persons …

Then I noticed the sprinklers spraying into the street, blasting at cars as startled drivers veered out of the line of fire and shook their fists at me. I hadn't adjusted the little doohickey things that set the parameters of the coverage pattern. So I grabbed a screwdriver and started randomly twisting adjustment screws as streams of water spewed willy-nilly in no discernible pattern. This went on for a very long time, and I was beginning to seriously rethink my career change when Dale ventured into the yard and suggested that I might want to consult the directions.

Isn't that just like a woman? A guy is out fixing something in a manly, manlike manner, and his wife wants to bog things down by reading a bunch of tiny words in some worthless little manual.

"I just need to calibrate the scapulators and reformat the gigahertzes and they will work fine," I said.

An hour later, soaking wet, I opened the instructions. The booklet explained exactly what I needed to do in the exact order in which I needed to do it. I followed the directions, and the sprinklers performed flawlessly. So I am ready to admit that instructions are invaluable, and they get more valuable the more complicated the subject. You and I can wing it and use our intuition on some things, but if we are going to assemble something complex, like an Air Force fighter jet, we will need a manual.

Likewise, when it comes to marriage (which is very complex even though it does not involve air-to-air missiles), we all desperately need instructions. We can learn a lot by playing the role of an apprentice, getting involved in a "marriage-mentor" relationship, and taking our cues from that. If our parents had good marriages, that can be a great way to learn. But we also need to familiarize ourselves with life's basic operating manual, the Bible. Although the Bible has much to say about the marriage relationship, it has even more to say about a vital, living, authentic relationship with God—the best foundation for a happy and successful marriage. God's own Spirit, overflowing with compassion and patience and kindness and all kinds of other great qualities, will empower each of us to be far greater spouses than we could ever hope to be on our own.

I have seen several on-the-rocks marriages dramatically transformed when spouses opened up their lives to God. This should not be surprising. Since God designed us to have personal and intimate relationships with Him, it only stands to reason that our other relationships will have deficits if we are missing that most essential of all relationships. We would not pump cranberry juice into our gas tanks, because our gasoline engines are not designed to run on anything other than gasoline. Likewise, if we try to run our lives on a power other than God's Spirit, it should not be terribly surprising when we sputter and stall.

All analogies break down about now, and that includes mine. I will therefore quickly state that there are many non-Christian couples who love each other deeply and have built deep and committed marriages. But I also assert that these couples are still missing out, because God designed marriage to include Him. As good as their marriages may be, they could be so much richer if the spouses made room for the Creator of love.

I know that some people roll their eyes at the very notion of the Bible being an authoritative manual for life. At one point in my life, I was one of those eye-rollers. The very idea can seem simplistic and hokey. Space does not permit me to launch into a lengthy explanation of why I now trust the Bible to be an accurate, authoritative, and relevant manual for life. That is not the purpose of this book. But I will say that powerful, well-reasoned books do address virtually any honest question you may want to pose. I highly recommend

Mere Christianity by C. S. Lewis as a starting point, and also *The Case for Christ* by Lee Strobel.

To simply dismiss the Bible as archaic or the mere writings of men without really studying the matter is intellectually dishonest and dangerous for your soul. Even if we can figure out a lot of stuff on our own, we need to admit that in some areas we are beyond our level of competence and understanding. We can't "wing it" with brain surgery, and we can't just "figure it out on our own" when it comes to God.

The Bible is a gift from God to the world. In it we find instructions we desperately need for all of our relationships, beginning with our relationships with Him. So, if you haven't yet cracked open the Maker's *Manual for Life*, there's no time like the present. (Personal bias: If you are a beginner, I think the best place to start is the gospel of John.)

Worst-Case Scenario

CHAPTER TWENTY-TWO

Several years ago, my wife bought our boys a book titled *The Worst-Case Scenario Survival Handbook.* It has short chapters that cover almost any extreme problem, ranging from "How to Escape from Quicksand" to "How to Escape from Killer Bees."

Not that my wife is a worrier. On the contrary, she is a hyper-worrier.

But she is no worse than 97.9 percent of other mothers, who seem genetically predisposed to assume that if their kids are more than an hour late getting back from the mall they have been in a horrible auto accident, been kidnapped, or been struck by a meteor. Or all three.

As a guy, when our boys were growing up, my default position was to assume that if one of them was late he had just lost track of time, forgotten to call, or gotten a flat tire on his bike. None of these scenarios involved calling the Missing Persons Bureau. (This is not to say that tardiness in our offspring does not matter. It does, because it is rude and irresponsible. I think it calls for appropriate, measured consequences so that it does not become a habit. But lateness does not require going to DEFCON 1.)

One woman in my wife's "Scrabble group" admits that when her boys were in college, if they were one hour late calling home she was already picking out the hymns for the funeral. Can you spell "n-e-u-r-o-t-i-c"?

All parents—both women *and* men—will inevitably worry about their kids. I think that reflects a protectiveness that God built into us. But we need to keep a sense of perspective, and we also need to take measured risks with our kids. They need to experience some risk as part of their maturing process.

When our boys were in first and third grade, I built a tree fort for them. In their fertile imaginations, it immediately became the lookout on a pirate ship. Initially, I had a ladder that led to their perch. That lasted a few hours; then the boys just wanted to climb the tree. Dale wanted them to use the ladder anyway. I told her that she needed to let them try climbing. It made her very nervous to watch them unsteadily move from branch to branch, but they did fine.

Climbing to the tree fort eventually led to climbing other trees, going waaaaaay out on a branch, and then leaping onto the roof of the house.

Dale was all twitchy about it.

I told them they could climb the trees, but I made them stay off the roof so they wouldn't tear up the shingles.

"I climbed trees when I was young, and I'm not dead yet," I pointed out to Dale. (She loves it when I use logic on her.)

The Bible has precisely zero to say on the subject of how high you should let your kid climb a tree. Or whether it is wise to have him play tackle football. Or what to say when your eighteen-year-old announces that he is going to try skydiving. And the odds are that men and women will have different comfort thresholds with all of these options. When Brad, at age seventeen, decided to get a moped (kind of a cross between a bike and a motorcycle), Dale was reduced to a bowl of quivering Jell-O every time he left the house. She could envision a score of awful scenarios—drunk or inattentive drivers, a slick spot in the road, an unexpected pothole, and on, and on, and on. None of these fears was unreasonable. Any traffic cop will tell you that riding a motorcycle dramatically increases your chances of serious injury or death in a collision. Yet, although I agreed with Dale about the risks, I was unwilling to forbid Brad to buy the moped.

"This is part of the letting-go process," I told Dale. "It makes me nervous, too. I understand the risk, but I don't feel like we should forbid it. I'll talk to him about the risks and about how to be safe. But we can't be nervous wrecks every day over this. I rode a motorcycle when I was his age, so what can I say?"

"You could tell him it was stupid," she said.

"But I still did it. And it isn't illegal or immoral. Just risky. And he is almost old enough to join the Marines. He is not our baby anymore."

If there was any plus to the moped, it was that it had a top speed of about forty miles per hour. Additionally, it gave us a huge new motivation to pray.

When Brad got his scuba-diving certification, it opened up yet another vista to get nervous about. When he signed up for his first ocean dive, Dale suddenly got cold feet. "We have no idea how competent the dive instructors are," she said. "They could be a fly-by-night outfit."

"Or felons, or drug lords, or Mafia dons," I said. "Hon,

the dive company is a big operation, and the hotel concierge suggested it."

"The concierge could be getting a kickback," she said.

So we randomly picked out a dive-equipment shop and wandered in. Dale asked the employee if he knew anything about the scam artists who were poised to dump our son into the ocean with a tank of substandard air that was probably imported from a polluted, third-world air basin.

"They are the best in the area," he replied.

Dale felt much better.

Same planet, different genders. It never would have occurred to me to double-check the bona fides of the dive instructors, who had been in business for years.

Because none of this stuff is subject to a "Thus-saith-the-Lord" announcement coming from an angel, it highlights yet one more of those areas in which husbands and wives are going to have to sort things out by talking, praying, and working out a compromise with each other.

Dale's more conservative, safety-conscious viewpoint has helped me to see potential problems I may have otherwise missed, and on many occasions I have set new limits or altered plans in direct response to her concerns. But on other occasions, I have convinced her that, as uncomfortable as it feels, she needs to bite her tongue and just let our kids undertake activities that make her nervous.

More than once I have reminded her, as she fretted about yet another way one of our sons could maim himself for life, that the little boys our kids grew up with have joined the army and are getting shot at in foreign deserts. Life has risks. We have to accept that. And pray a lot.

Investing for the Long Haul

CHAPTER TWENTY-THREE

I have no background or formal training in financial matters, but over the years I have wisely invested in a commodity that lasts about one week, then loses all of its economic value and gets tossed into the trash. I am not talking about stock in an Internet start-up company. I am talking about flowers.

Specifically, I am talking about flowers given on September 8, or June 30, or any non-holiday, non-birthday, non-anniversary, or other non-occasion. I am talking about surprise flowers that are connected to nothing but the desire to surprise and delight. Giving your wife surprise flowers— or any thoughtful gift—is an unspoken message that lets her know you were thinking about her, that you went out of your way to please her, and that she is special to you.

I buy flowers at the grocery store. Unlike the typical florist shop, where a bouquet of flowers can cost as much as the down payment on a car, grocery store flowers cost me no more than a couple of boxes of Froot Loops. You don't have to buy a dozen expensive roses to brighten your wife's day. Simpler flowers are great, too.

When I am checking out of the store with a bouquet of flowers, there is a striking difference in the typical reaction between male and female cashiers.

FEMALE CHECKER: "Oh, those are so beautiful! She'll love them. Special occasion?"

MALE CHECKER: "What did you do wrong?"

Many men give flowers after doing something stupid, like forgetting an anniversary or, worse, forgetting an anniversary and also inviting a bunch of guys over to watch game four of the World Series that evening.

Can you spell "i-d-i-o-t"? Although buying flowers to emphasize an apology is not a bad idea, you don't want to inextricably connect flowers to acts of stupidity. If you only give flowers to say you are sorry, every time your wife sees a rose bush or a field of poppies she will be reminded about the time you promised to pick up dog food on the way home from work, but you forgot so you fed the dog a burrito instead and the entire family had to sleep in the backyard until the house finally aired out.

You need to give flowers that are not an apology, not intended to get you out of the doghouse, and not a belated gift to make up for forgetting or missing an important event. Flowers are an investment in your marriage, and they pay dividends that far, far, far exceed their cost. When Dale comes home and sees fresh flowers on the dining room table or the kitchen counter, her smile is simply priceless. Even her eyes smile.

Dale loves the beauty of flowers, but that is just half of the story. She would not have nearly the same reaction if the flowers were the result of winning the "free-flowers-for-a-year" drawing from the Amalgamated Florists of America. No, the joy comes from the fact that I, her husband, gave them to her. Each time I give her flowers, it is a colorful way of saying, "I still do."

I have never met a woman who said, "Oh, I enjoyed getting flowers while I was dating my future husband. But now I think they are frivolous, wasteful, and unnecessary."

Guys, if our wives enjoyed being wooed when we were dating, they will enjoy being wooed twenty years later. In a world where so many marriages fail, doesn't it make sense for us to keep doing the thoughtful little things we did back when we wanted to tell them in a hundred different ways that they matter to us?

Sadly, men often slowly but surely drift away from all those little acts that mean so much to women. I don't think it is necessarily because guys are inherently dunderheads or uncaring. I think it could be, in part, a reflection of the fact that things that are meaningful to women are often not the same things that are meaningful to men. Dale has never given me flowers, or teacups, or little craft items. There is a reason for this. I would not like them. That stuff does not make me tick. Because this stuff is kind of foreign to us, we guys may need to remind ourselves that it matters to our spouses. This may mean that we need to hide this note to ourselves in our cars or at work: "Note to self: Do something romantic."

If you are not the spontaneous type, *plan* to be spontaneous. Get a computer program that emails reminders to you. The danger of familiarity is that it can breed a dullness, a rut, a stale predictability. This can happen in our relationships with our spouses and even in our relationships with God.

Indeed, Jesus warned the Ephesian church, "You have forsaken your first love" (Revelation 2:4).

His remedy? "Do the things you did at first" (Revelation 2:5).

Feeling Sheepish

CHAPTER TWENTY-FOUR

When I was just a lad, my grandmother taught me helpful axioms about life, such as, "The grass is always greener someplace, so don't cry over spilled milk." I had no clue what she was talking about, but she baked great goodies, so I happily nibbled on oatmeal-raisin cookies while she told me not to count my chickens while two of them were still in the bush. It took me years to untangle such metaphors, but I eventually learned that there is a lot of truth packed into those wise sayings.

The grass on the other side of the fence often does look greener, which is a simple way of saying that we can feel tempted to bolt from our current situations and jump into new fields that we think will make us happier. Single people often desperately wish they were married, but married people can find themselves longing for those "carefree" days when they were single.

When I was single, I shared a house with four single guys. We were pathetic. We pressed our little sheep bodies against the fence of wedded bliss and emitted pitiable bleating sounds as we watched all the married sheep having picnics over in the great, green fields of matrimony. Sure, we had all kinds of freedom and disposable income and virtually no responsibilities in our fields of singleness, but we were also lonely. And twitchy. We wanted to be married, and the only barrier was that we had not quite found the right women to marry. We wanted the love and companionship and joy—and let's not forget sex—that are inherent in a good marriage.

All of us finally found great women and are happily married. But I think it is normal that sometimes—when finances get tight, or when the kids are acting up, or when the washing machine conks out—married people can get a sudden longing for the days when they could do virtually whatever they wanted to do. We married sheep find our dismal little sheep faces pressed against the fence of singleness as we watch all the unmarried sheep buying motorcycles, dating other sheep, and, if they are guys, drinking milk straight out of the carton.

Thus the spectacle continues as two flocks of sheep on opposite sides of the fence cast longing glances at each other's fields, feeling a bit jealous and perhaps even a bit bitter because the other side seems to have it better.

It's just sheep nature. It's also stupid. The fact is that both singleness and marriage have distinct advantages and disadvantages. When I was single, one enormous opportunity I enjoyed was time. I had gobs of time to read novels, study my Bible, take cheap trips to cool places, engage in significant ministry, form deep and lasting friendships, develop photos in my darkroom, and do just about whatever I wanted.

Instead of bemoaning their singleness, unmarried folks should seize the opportunity to live life to its fullest while single. Besides, if you want to attract a mate, you are much more likely to succeed if you are happy and self-confident rather than desperate and clingy.

That said, marriage has immense joys that are not found in single life. I get to live with the person I most love. I don't wake up alone. My wife and I cherish our little routines: coffee together every morning, favorite restaurants, romantic evenings by our fireplace. We have purposeful and important work that we do together: raising a family, ministering as a team, supporting and encouraging each other in good times and in bad.

Despite all the benefits of marriage, all of us married folks need to understand that we will at some point feel an impulse to scamper over to where the grass seems greener. But the desire to bolt to other pastures is always a bad temptation. That desire to get our "freedom" back is particularly dangerous when it is not merely a wistful and passing feeling but is tied to a specific person.

If you are daydreaming about how That Other Person could *really* make you happy, unlike the Person You Married, you are on a dangerous path. If you are in regular contact with That Other Person, such as in a work situation, the danger is intensified. If you are flirting, you are in the spiritual equivalent of a burning building, and you need to dash to the nearest exit.

The grass is not greener inside the flaming warehouse. And the fact that when we are tempted to be unfaithful we seldom recognize that we are in a flaming warehouse indicates just how morally blind and desensitized we can be.

Left unnurtured, marriage can become a difficult, draining, and even painful relationship. It can range from being simply boring to intensely caustic. Not surprisingly, many people want to run from such painful relationships. That other grass looks waaaaaay greener, indeed.

But if you are tempted to flee a marriage, let me give you both a warning and a hope. First, God tells us in the Bible that He hates divorce. He intends for us to make a lifelong vow to our spouses and keep it. That's the warning.

Second, there is hope for a troubled, wounded, damaged marriage. Even yours. It might not seem possible, but it is true. The same God who tells us to stay married—for better or for worse, in sickness and in health—also promises to give us the resources we need to make our marriages places of renewal, joy, and healing.

In Isaiah 42:3, God promises not to snuff out a "smoldering wick." The marital flame can be rekindled. I have seen marriages saved that were clearly, swiftly, and from all appearances inexorably heading toward disaster. I have marveled to see wounds healed, sins forgiven, and souls knit back together by what can only be described as a supernatural act.

But we have to be open to that process. We need to cooperate with God. I'm reminded of the time Jesus told a man with a withered hand, "Stretch out your hand" (Matthew 12:13).

Uh, Jesus, he *couldn't* stretch out his hand! That was his problem!

But the man cooperated with Jesus. As he did that which he could not do, he was restored while in the very process of answering Jesus' seemingly impossible request.

So, how do we cooperate with God to improve and even restore our marriages? We start with the decision to obey God's revealed will, whether or not we feel like it. We grit our teeth and decide not to hop the fence. But we don't stop there. We then let God work on us, no matter how painful it may be. And one of God's primary ways of working on us is through other people. So, like it or not, we will need to seek help and tell the truth.

If your marriage needs help, or even a "miracle," say this aloud to yourself: "I need help to rescue my marriage." Then say it to a wise, experienced marriage counselor or a healthy married couple in your church. Tell a pastor what you are facing. Call a friend. This problem is bigger than you and your spouse, and you need to reach out. If your spouse won't reach out with you, go first. Take the step that has to be taken. Stretch out that withered hand.

Let me throw in a caveat: Everything I have written thus far presumes a certain level of normalcy in a marriage, even if a marriage is troubled. That is, I am assuming that a couple may have been growing apart, feeling cold toward each other, or feeling hurt, dry inside, and emotionally wrung out. But I am not assuming danger, violence, or deep deviancy (like the guy who brought home his girlfriend to join in the "marriage"). In situations that are clearly beyond the bounds of "troubled but normal," you need to go someplace safe. God does not intend for you to be abused or dragged into someone else's perversion of everything He intends marriage to be. You still need to reach out for help, but don't labor under the thought that you have a unilateral responsibility to "save your marriage." That can't be done by you alone. It takes two to make a marriage, and it takes two to keep a marriage going.

I actually know of a man who was quite willing to stay in his marriage as long as his wife accepted the fact that he fully intended to keep his mistress. That was the "deal" he offered her. She wisely declined the offer. *She* did not dissolve the marriage. He did. She simply filed the paperwork that ratified his decision. But most troubled marriages are not facing this kind of crisis. And most marriages can be saved if the couples involved will make that tough decision to work through the issues no matter what.

Remember, once you and I said, "I do," we closed the gate to the other pastures. Each of us must focus on making our marriages work. God Himself is pulling for us.

I think my grandma would agree with my axiom: "A bird in hand is better than a bird in a flaming warehouse."

Synchronized Flailing

Dale and I were standing on the lakeshore with eight other couples, listening intently as a park ranger gave us instructions on how to maneuver a two-person kayak without maiming someone else. He told us how to hold the paddle, how to synchronize our movements, how to steer, and what to do if the kayak flipped over. Then he asked, "Are any of you married to the person who will be in the boat with you?"

Several of us raised our hands.

"We'll have marriage counseling available when we get back to shore," he said.

We all laughed. I mean, how hard could this be?

"Okay, we need the heaviest persons to get into the rear seats," he said.

"That would be you," Dale whispered helpfully.

"The person in the rear does the steering, but the person in the front sets the pace," the ranger continued.

My job would be to match my strokes to Dale's, varying

my rhythm only to steer. An extra stroke on the right side of the kayak would nudge us to the left and vice versa.

Soon we put our kayaks into the lake, settled into our positions, and put the paddles into the water. With our guide leading the way, our group began paddling across the lake in a relatively synchronized manner. Well, at least most of our group.

As the majority of our flotilla glided across the water, one kayak was a spectacle of flailing oars, splashing water, and mutually contradictory actions. The husband looked as if he were either trying to set a world speed record or escape a hive of enraged bees. He was paying *zero* attention to the rhythm of his wife's strokes, and their paddles crashed together constantly as they zigzagged across the water, occasionally ramming other kayaks. It looked like the guy was deliberately doing the exact opposite of every single piece of guidance the ranger had given us ten minutes earlier. The only time he ceased thrashing was when he got so tired that he had to rest. Then he would pause a few moments while his wife paddled without him (making far more progress than when he was "helping"), and then he would thrash wildly once again.

One goal of the kayak tour was to quietly approach the local wildlife—deer, bears, storks, rabbits—and observe them as our ranger pointed them out using hand signals. But our group approached with all the stealth of an armored tank division firing every single round of available ammunition. I think the wildlife is still stampeding toward Quebec.

What can we, as married persons, learn from this episode? (Reader warning: Dave will now employ a horrendous, dreadful metaphor in order to make his point. Persons majoring in English may need to seek medical assistance.)

Clearly, we must learn to synchronize the paddles of cooperation as we journey on the lake of matrimony, or we risk driving the wildlife of wedded bliss into the wilderness of conflict, where it will be mauled by the grizzly bear of spousal hostility. (I am tempted to add a line about the virtuous turtle of patience being trampled by the angry elk of noncooperation, but the code of federal regulations forbids the reckless and willful abuse of moralistic metaphors.)

Okay, so I'm not Shakespeare. But even the bard would agree with my essential point—married partners need to be paddling in the same direction or their marriages will be chaotic.

Consider this real-life scenario: After several years of marriage, he (adventuresome soul) decides he wants to be a missionary and serve God in a distant land. She (risk-averse, hates bugs, values stability) most emphatically does not want to become a missionary. Against her wishes, he plows ahead with his plan. The marriage ends in divorce. The question is not whether he was more spiritual or whether she was too timid. It is not whether he was truly "called" to the mission field. The question is whether they were united in this major decision, and the answer is clearly "no." Matrimonial paddles were banging, water was splashing, and animals were running for cover as the couple paddled vigorously in opposite directions.

If you are in a one-person kayak, you can go wherever you want. You don't need to coordinate with anyone. You get to steer, and you set the pace. That all changes when it becomes a two-person adventure.

I regularly witness major stupidity pursued under the guise of one spouse invoking "God's will." "I'm just following God's will," spouts the bullheaded spouse as he or she drags a reluctant partner along. I am deeply suspicious of a person who glibly claims a special insight into the will of God, and my suspicion is compounded tenfold when the person's spouse is sending signals of quiet desperation or vocal opposition.

There are a lot of things I don't know about the will of God, but I do know that He does not want me to wreck my marriage. He does not want me to run roughshod over Dale's opinions or desires; He does not want me to be stubborn; He does not want me to be insensitive; and He certainly does not want me to make major, unilateral decisions for both of us and call it "leadership." If you think you are leading and you look behind you and no one is following, you are not leading but merely enjoying a stroll.

Let's say a guy named Ted is a schoolteacher and decides that he really wants to be a member of the police SWAT team. That desire is not right or wrong; it is merely a preference. If Ted is single, he prays about it and maybe even seeks advice, but in the end he decides. It is extremely unlikely that an angel will show up and announce the will of God concerning Ted's decision. Indeed, I think God gives Ted—and all of us— huge amounts of latitude in our decisions about life. He offers broad moral parameters and lets us make choices. So becoming a bookie or a Mafia hit man is off the table when it comes to acceptable occupations for Ted, but zillions of other options are open to him. But if Ted is married, he gives up the right to unilaterally pursue any dream that attracts him. Because he and his spouse, Ellen, have been joined as "one," Ted's career decision needs to be a joint decision.

Continuing this illustration, let's say that Ted and Ellen discuss Ted's radical career change. They consider the inherent dangers of being on a SWAT team. They pray about it and research it, and Ellen decides to fully support Ted's desire. She knows that she will face daily concern about his safety, but she is also proud of him for taking on a job that must be done. That's a green light for Ted to proceed.

But let's suppose that Ellen, whose father was killed in the line of duty as an officer with the highway patrol, simply can't deal with the dangers and uncertainties that Ted wants to pursue. She begs him not to join the SWAT team. In this case, Ted would be an idiot to go down that road. I'll go out on a limb here and venture to say it would violate God's will to pursue the SWAT team career because it would clearly put the marriage at risk.

Let's consider one more permutation of the scenario. Suppose Ted was already a member of the SWAT team when he started dating Ellen. And let's suppose she understood that he was passionate about his work, and he received a great deal of satisfaction from his career in public safety. It would be profoundly unfair for Ellen to marry him and then start complaining about his job. In that case, Ellen, not Ted, would be damaging the marriage.

My point is that each of us and our respective spouses make up a team that needs to paddle together. But even when we are pulling in the same direction, when we are trying to cooperate, when we are paddling in unison, when we are doing our very best, we still face powerful forces that threaten to blow us off course or even sink us.

Our park ranger noted that a week before our kayak adventure, a group of boaters was in the middle of a moonlight tour when a nasty storm hit the lake. Whitecaps slapped against the boats, one vessel capsized, and the group eventually had to radio in for a rescue. They were doing their best, but their best was not equal to the forces of nature arrayed against them. Jesus' disciples found themselves in that situation as they sailed on a lake during a vicious storm. They tried to get safely to shore, but the wind was howling and things looked pretty grim. Then Jesus came walking across the water and met them in their distress. When He climbed into the boat, "the wind died down" (Matthew 14:32).

So let's paddle in unity with our spouses and invite Jesus into our boats.

Rounding Up the Weeds

CHAPTER TWENTY-SIX

I pulled weeds this morning. I pulled weeds last week. A couple weeks ago, I nuked vast sectors of our yard with weed killer, and today waist-high dead weeds grace the border of our backyard fence. If you need some extra weeds, I have oodles that you can harvest for free.

I am the designated sprayer of dangerous chemicals in our family. I also take care of anything related to fixing the cars. (Typically, this means I hand large sums of cash to the mechanic while I pretend to understand anything he just said about the injectors, the manifold, the reactor core, or the hemoglobin.)

Dale is the designated maker of German chocolate cakes. She also sews on any errant buttons. We mutually agreed on this arrangement years ago. But when I manfully agreed that I would bravely unleash destruction and woe upon the weeds, Dale warned me that if I let them go for even a short period of time, they would multiply with a vengeance.

To my credit, there were legitimate reasons not to spray

during the course of the past few months. Some days it was too windy, and I didn't want to waft weed killer into the air and wipe out every shrub in the neighborhood and be chased down the street by elderly, enraged members of the local garden club, who would whap me upside the head with their trowels.

Some days it was just too hot. I have always believed that sweating is a sign of poor manners, so I carefully limit my outdoor exertions. Other days it was a bit nippy, and I didn't want to risk applying the weed killer at less than the ideal temperature.

"What is the ideal temperature?" Dale asked in her transparently skeptical tone.

"The same as inside the mall," I replied.

Other days there were mechanics to pay, errands to run, or other difficult chores to do, such as picking up the newspaper in order to read the comics.

I would prefer to not have weeds at all, but if I do have to deal with them, I would prefer to do it at times that work for me. So, the end result was that, in spite of all my perfectly good reasons for not dispatching the weeds while they were small, the nasty little plants positively erupted like Jack's beanstalk on steroids.

Weeds are like that. They are inconsiderate and pushy and rude, and they refuse to stay put until an appropriate and convenient day comes around for me to deal with them. If weeds had the ability to talk, they would merely scoff at me in their weedy little voices. "Neener, neener, neener!" they would say flippantly, as they choked the geraniums and strangled the hydrangeas.

Our yard is now infested with a weed called wild morning glory. Very invasive, it puts out long tentacles that wrap around other plants and throttle the chlorophyll right out of them. Once a morning glory tentacle has spiraled up the stalk of another plant, it is extremely difficult to remove it. You literally have to unwind each tentacle. If you simply rip it out at the roots, you almost always rip up the plant you are trying to rescue.

"Let this be a lesson to you," I told Dale. "If we had simply pulled up these weeds when they were small, or sprayed them earlier, we wouldn't be breaking our backs dealing with them now." (Dale loves it when I give her valuable gardening tips. Often, she is so awed by my insights that she is unable to speak for twenty minutes.)

To be perfectly truthful, I have a tendency to ignore weeds until they become so aggressive that they have worked their way into the house and begun placing expensive, long-distance telephone calls to Bermuda in order to invite all the grass over for a party.

Regrettably, weeds, like other problems, do not typically just go away if we ignore them. In the short-term, it is "easier" to ignore little weeds in our yards—and lives. Dealing with weeds takes time and energy, and often we feel like we have no time or energy to spare. It takes work to solve problems, and we already feel overworked. So we are tempted to let things slide.

But problems left alone tend to deepen, take root, and grow worse.

No gardener has ever faced the dilemma of ripping out the tomatoes, the pumpkin vines, or the zucchini plants because they were crowding out the weeds. No, if you leave your garden alone for a few weeks, all the good plants will be struggling to survive against the onslaught of the weeds.

Garden-variety weeds aren't the only ones that demand

our attention, though. The Bible cautions us, "See to it that no one misses the grace of God and that no bitter root grows up to cause trouble and defile many" (Hebrews 12:15). Bitterness, anger, selfishness, greed, and other nasty "weeds" need to be nuked, pulled up, and tossed into the trash. It can be very tough to even admit that these noxious plants have taken root in our lives or in the lives of our spouses. But we simply can't afford to ignore these weeds or they will take over and dominate our lives.

It was not easy, for example, for Dale to point out, firmly but lovingly, that I was developing a serious problem with anger. Why, the very accusation indignated my righteousness! My first response was to justify my increasingly frequent outbursts of anger. I had excellent reasons to be angry. There were problems, issues, dilemmas, predicaments, quandaries, pressures, and let's not forget dire straits that were all converging to shorten my temper. I was working too many hours, the kids weren't behaving, finances were tight ... I had all kinds of excuses.

"Until you view your behavior as a sin, you will not be able to overcome it," Dale said.

Sin? Ouch.

It was not easy for Dale to say those brutally honest, precisely on-target words. She does not like conflict. But she saw anger really taking root in my life and was determined to tackle the issue head-on.

I did not repent on the spot. In fact, I was defensive. I was upset that she had the audacity to tell *me* that *I* was the problem. (There is nothing that makes a man angrier than having someone point out that he has an anger problem.) But Dale's words stuck with me, and once I was calm enough to be rational, I had to face the fact that she was right. I was engaging in outbursts of anger—a clear violation of the warning found in 2 Corinthians 12:20—and there was no excuse for it.

Jesus was confronted with problems, issues, dilemmas, and pressures far worse than anything I've ever encountered, but He did not become a shouting, raving idiot. He didn't blow up and then say, "Well, that's just my temperament" or, "The devil made me do it."

Dale helped me squarely face the harsh fact that the anger weed was growing fast in me. But acknowledging the problem is not the same as fixing the problem. Noticing the weeds is an important first step, but the noticing has to be followed up by the hard work of doing something about them.

I have not resolved my anger problem once and for all. I still become too angry, too fast, too easily. But by the grace of God, and with Dale's help, I am working on it instead of excusing it.

All gardeners understand that even if you completely rid a garden of weeds, it is only a brief victory. They always come back. But a smart gardener is vigilant and active, not allowing destructive plants to thrive. Sometimes what looks to you like a flower looks to your wife like a weed. Trust your spouse. It's a weed.

Dave's Shortest Chapter Ever

CHAPTER TWENTY-SEVEN

Follow the logic here:

1. Marriage is a gift God has given to humanity.

2. A spouse should be viewed, therefore, as a gift from God.

Why is it, then, that if I come home from work and announce, "Hi, Hon! God's gift to you is here!" Dale tends to roll her eyes and make droll comments that do not sound particularly grateful?

The Power of Believing in Your Spouse

CHAPTER TWENTY-EIGHT

The main reason I am a published writer can be summed up in one word: *my wife*. (Okay, I know "my wife" is technically two words. So sue me. I was an English major, not a math guy.)

Several years ago, I really wanted to attend a writers' conference. I wanted a chance to meet editors face–to-face. I wanted the opportunity to submit my manuscript to the folks who could make a decision about it. But as I weighed the opportunity against the cost, I didn't know if I could justify attending. I was still paying off an automobile transmission that had conked out months earlier, so I didn't have extra cash sitting around. If I spent the money, took the trip, and didn't sell the manuscript, I'd feel like an idiot.

"I've decided not to go," I told Dale.

"You're going," she replied.

"We don't have the money," I said.

"We have the money," she answered.

And we did—because she had saved it up one painstaking dollar at a time for months. Because she believed in me.

Dale was working half-days as a reading aide at a school. But she had also quietly taken on extra duties, like working in the lunchroom for an extra thirty minutes a day. Cleaning up spills and scraping gum off tables was not glamorous work, but she did it because the extra money would be enough to send me to the event.

"But we can pay off bills," I said.

"The only thing we will spend the money on is sending you," she replied.

She believed in me. She believed I was worth the investment. Even if my manuscript was rejected, she considered every dime well spent.

So I went. I stayed in the cheapest dorm room I could get, and my roommate snored like a Husqvarna chainsaw, but I was there. I took every class and workshop I could possibly cram into my schedule. I met editors. I stayed up until absurd hours of the night commiserating with other would-be writers. And, nervous but hopeful, I submitted my material for consideration.

And someone decided to publish my book. Then another one. And another one. And yet another one.

The book you are holding is my fifth, and more are in the pipeline. And it all started because my wife not only believed in me but went out of her way to help me succeed. She sacrificed. She put me first. She did all she could to set me up for success.

Now it is my turn to help her pursue some dreams. Early in our married life, Dale set aside a host of other options so she could focus on raising our boys. She did the hard work of being a mom. It is a role that is profoundly underappreciated in today's society, but she and I both grasped the importance of her being there for our kids, especially when they were younger. Now that our sons are older, Dale is exploring her options, and I have the privilege of doing all I can to help her realize her goals.

It is important for husbands and wives to look for ways to help each other achieve their potential in all areas of life. We need to nurture each other spiritually, emotionally, intellectually, and physically. We need to set each other up for success. We need to foster each other's dreams.

A couple of years ago, I dropped by the corporate office of an old friend I had not seen in a few years. His name is Dave, and two decades ago we did some ministry work together for a high school youth group.

The receptionist informed me that Dave was no longer with the company.

Oh.

That didn't sound good. Dave was a pretty senior guy in the office the last time I had seen him. "Any idea where he is?" I asked.

"He sells tractors," replied the receptionist.

Oh.

From executive in a big corporation to tractor salesman. That did not sound good.

It is a long story, but Dale and I eventually found ourselves pulling up to the rural farm home of Dave and his lovely wife, Carla. I could see a small shop with a partially dismantled tractor in it. A sign hung over the shop: "Dave's Tractors."

Dave walked toward us with a wide grin on his face. We exchanged small talk for a few minutes; then I asked what happened. Still smiling, Dave replied, "I found myself hating my job. The money was good, but the hours were so long. I was stretched too thin. We kept having corporate restructures, and everyone had to essentially reapply for his or her position each time. I kept getting my job back but found myself almost wishing I hadn't."

He and Carla talked it over. She did not want him working at a job he had begun to loathe. It was a huge risk, but they took every dime they had and bought tractors.

"I figured that if we could sell a few tractors a month, we could make it," he told me.

"And how's it going?" I asked, bracing myself for the answer.

Dave looked me in the eye and replied, "Amazing. We've been at it for two years, and we're doing a couple million dollars in sales each year."

Over pizza and iced tea, Dave talked about his plans for his large, new shop. He is having the time of his life, and it is largely because his wife believed in him and blessed his unorthodox and wholly unconventional idea. It didn't hurt that Dave is a bright guy, a natural salesman, and a good mechanic. But he also needed the support of his wife, and Carla was there for him.

That story has a happy ending. But sometimes the business fizzles, the plan falls apart, the project flames out. What then?

Dale and I have friends who operated a successful travel agency but lost everything when an international political incident resulted in mass cancellations for a tour and a charter flight they had already booked and paid for. The circumstances could not have been foreseen and were wholly beyond their control. They basically lost everything except each other—but they still have each other, and that is the most important thing. They did not let calamity drive them apart. They still believe in each other and remain committed to each other.

Sometimes we guys generate cockamamie ideas that no rational person should support, especially not our wives. Zeal does not trump solid, rational planning. And no spouse should simply roll ahead with a plan that is not supported by his or her mate. I have seen this played out, and it is not a pretty picture.

"Jack" had a high-risk business plan that would require all his time and pay no income unless and until it succeeded. His spouse was a full-time mom who cared for their young children. She thought Jack's idea was untenable and unwise, but it was his dream, so he simply plowed ahead despite her concerns. There was no margin for error. It is one thing to take a calculated risk together. It is quite another to force a huge risk on a reluctant or unwilling spouse. Jack's plan never panned out, and his family will be paying the price— both financially and emotionally—for many years to come.

Jack didn't simply make an unwise financial decision. He made an arrogant decision. His unspoken and yet clear message to his wife was, "Your opinion and your concerns don't matter to me." If Jack's wife had been fully supportive of the decision, the outcome would have been quite different, even if the plan still failed.

You cannot make your spouse believe in you. Trust is something you earn over time in hundreds of little ways. But when you have it, and when the day comes that you need to make a big jump, there is nothing quite as exhilarating as having your mate willingly take your hand, look you in the eye, and say, "I believe in you, no matter how this turns out. Let's go."

Routine Maintenance

"Maintaining a marriage isn't like maintaining my '71 Bronco. With my Bronco, all I had to do was check the air filter a couple times each year, keep the fluids topped off, and it was fine for months."

This insightful comment came from a guy named Mark, who was commenting on what he had learned after eight months of marriage. (Note: Mark's day job does not involve writing inspirational messages for greeting cards.) He shared his observation during a church-related, small-group event for couples. Although it was not the most poetic comparison in the world, Mark's comment was nevertheless fairly accurate. A '71 Bronco does require regular tune-ups and tire rotations, but it never gets its feelings hurt and never asks you if its new spark plugs clash with the carburetor. But even a sport utility vehicle, left unattended, will rust, fall apart, and get ruined. Clearly, Mark's Bronco is still running more than thirty years after it rolled off the assembly line because it received regular oil changes, tune-ups, brake jobs, and other attention.

If a mechanical object requires routine care to preserve it, how much more care do our spouses need? Virtually all of us regularly see unmaintained marriages parked on the side of life's freeway, smoking and steaming and needing to be towed in for massive repairs. Tragically, the average marriage today lasts about seven years—far less than the average car. And, unfortunately, an unmaintained marriage, just like a neglected automobile, can look okay outwardly for quite some time before it shudders to a stop.

Many years ago, a friend of mine had a nice-looking Volkswagen Beetle that she drove and drove and drove without changing the oil. Occasionally she added some oil, but she did not quite grasp the concept of actually changing it. So the oil, which was hardening into a dense, tar-like substance, had all the lubricating properties of sandpaper while she drove and drove and drove. The car looked perfectly okay, until one day the engine suddenly croaked. Never had an engine suffered so much for so long. It gave all it could have possibly given, but it was simply ruined by neglect.

My friend was not trying to ruin her car. She did not deliberately abuse it. She didn't pour sugar into the gas tank or bash the doors with a sledgehammer or—worse—loan it to her sixteen-year-old brother. She simply failed to give the car routine care.

Are you maintaining your marriage? Let's run through the basic checklist:

Fluids: You need to prevent the buildup of friction in your marriage. The Bible mentions something called the "oil of gladness" (Isaiah 61:3). I don't know exactly what it is, but I like the concept. How's the gladness level in your marriage?

What can you do to add to it? Think about something that would make your spouse glad—and do it. Has there been a specific point of friction, something that has been wearing on your spouse? What can you do, in a practical way, to ease or even eliminate the problem?

Spark plugs: How's the spark in your marriage? What are you doing to keep romance in your life? When is the last time you gave your husband a love note out of the blue, for no reason? Why not make your wife a bubble bath, light some scented candles, and offer a complete head-to-toe massage? The possibilities are endless.

Battery: Sometimes your "relationship battery" gets drained and needs to be recharged. It isn't that the battery is bad; it has just been sapped of all its energy. One of the best ways to reenergize your relationship is to get away for awhile—just the two of you. This can be hard sometimes, especially if you have young children at home. But try to work out something. An overnight trip can do wonders for a tired couple. One bleak December day, I took Dale to a bed-and-breakfast just an hour's drive away. Time seemed to slow down as we were transported to a different, romantic world. God even arranged for it to snow, which was very nice of Him. We got to sit by the window, listen to soft "big-band" music, and watch the puffy flakes float softly to the ground. It was exactly what we needed.

Earlier in our marriage, when we were very broke, we took inexpensive day trips and short camping trips. If you can't get away overnight, you can still manage to get away for the evening. Make it a priority. Make it happen. All marriages need to be recharged.

Brakes: Sometimes life starts moving too fast, and you need to be able to slow it down. Are too many activities crammed into your week? Are you chronically tired? You need some brake work. Dale mentioned to me recently that a family we know has something going on almost every night of the week on a regular basis. That is a crash waiting to happen. Even "good" activities cease to be good if they keep you in a frenzy of motion. And don't keep doing activities out of guilt. It is disturbingly common to see couples who are "active in church" suddenly divorce. Maybe they were a little too active. We all need quality time with our spouses. And quality time is not something we can cram in on the fly. We won't have quality time without quantity time. Make sure your brakes are functioning, and use them.

Fuel: Jesus said that we don't live by bread alone but by the Word of God (see Matthew 4:4). The Scriptures are a source of supernatural fuel for our hearts and souls—and our marriages. Even if we have already taken care of the items listed earlier, recharged batteries and functional brakes don't do much if our fuel tanks are empty. The Bible repeatedly and emphatically says that we need God's Word in our lives. In a mysterious process we don't really grasp, when we "fill up" on God's Word, His Spirit transforms that Word into a super-natural fuel that helps us to be more loving, patient, kind, and wise. We need this as individuals, and also as married couples. If the Bible is not a current part of the routine main-tenance of your marriage, make it so.

If we do all of the above "maintenance," our marriages won't be like struggling little Volkswagens with paralyzed engines. They will be like high-performance models that carry us to the finish line with style, grace, and joy.

You Are in the War Zone

Night had fallen by the time I drove up to the barricaded entrance of Edwards Air Force Base in Southern California. As one of the heavily armed airmen approached my vehicle, he glanced down at the recently expired Air Force identification sticker affixed to my bumper. His eyes widened for a moment as he counted the stripes, and he stood a bit more erect as he approached my window.

"Sir, are you a retired master sergeant?" he asked with a touch of awe in his voice.

(For those of you who are not familiar with the military, I need to explain that anyone who achieves the rank of master sergeant is a rare breed and garners considerable respect among the brotherhood of soldiers.)

I would have spent a few minutes chatting modestly about my many dangerous experiences were it not for the fact that the most daring feat I had performed during the past decade was replacing an electrical outlet in the kitchen.

"Sorry," I replied. "I bought the car used, and a previous owner was in the Air Force."

"Oh," he replied, clearly disappointed.

There was an awkward silence for a moment. Then he added, "You really should remove that from your bumper."

"I tried, but it is a plastic bumper and the sticker is really fused on," I said.

"Maybe we can scrape it off," he said helpfully, pulling out a pocketknife and scratching it across the bumper to no avail.

"See what I mean?" I said.

"Yeah, but maybe you can cover it up with something," he replied.

He was kindly diplomatic, but I was already translating his comment into this: "It wouldn't really be right if someone mistook you for a professional soldier when the most aggressive thing you do on any given day is flail your barbecue mitt at the meat bees when you are cooking burgers."

"Good idea," I replied. "Thanks."

I filled out all the visitor information forms and felt miserably safe as the guard waved me past the barricades. Soon I arrived at the home of my brother-in-law, who is a real Air Force sergeant who flies around in real Air Force planes, goes on real missions, stands in the open doorway of a gargantuan C-130, and gets combat pay for entering hostile air space.

I've never been shot at. I've never thrown a grenade, even in practice. Although I've been yelled at a few times, it was never by someone in uniform, unless you count a Little League coach.

I think that, deep down, all guys want to be warriors. We want to be engaged in an epic battle where the stakes are high and where we *matter*. Where we rush the hill that *must* be taken. Where we can be heroes.

We can.

God has called us to be warriors, even if we never pick up a gun. That stuff the apostle Paul wrote about putting on the "full armor of God, so that … you may be able to stand your ground" (Ephesians 6:13) was not a poetic flourish. There really is a battle raging, and we really are in the thick of it.

The world is launching a barrage of missiles at marriages and families. These weapons are spiritual and invisible, but we see the casualties all around us. There are so many wounded spouses, so many hurting children. When I confronted a friend who was about to ruin his marriage, I was participating in the battle. When I offered friendship, hope, and advice to a man struggling with the temptation of an affair, I was holding some ground. When Dale and I pray for our kids, we are actively repelling the enemy.

Early in their marriage, Dale's parents served in the Salvation Army. This organization is structured like a military force, with officers and even uniforms. The battle her parents fought was a spiritual one, but no less real than any other battle fought in human history.

I am a soldier, and so are you. And we are in the greatest battle of the biggest war imaginable. And you *matter*.

It's Only Money

CHAPTER THIRTY-ONE

I don't understand why "disagreement over finances" consistently rates as one of the key problems married couples face, especially when the Visa people have thoughtfully arranged a system whereby we can keep spending and spending even when we don't have any money. What's to disagree over? It's basically like having unlimited cash. I don't know why my wife can't grasp this self-evident fact.

Credit cards are tremendously convenient. I have a gob of them in my wallet (and even more of them in my dresser drawer), and the U.S. Postal Service brings me a new batch of offers almost daily. In many cases, the credit card companies offer to give me a bunch of free stuff if I just agree to use their cards.

"Hey, look!" I called to Dale one day as I brought in the mail. "We got a credit card application from an airline. We can earn free tickets to anywhere if we just charge some stuff! I think I'll sign us up."

"It's a scam, just like the scam about getting money

toward a car," Dale replied. "Read the fine print, and you'll discover that you have to buy $100,000.00 worth of stuff at a noncompetitive interest rate to get a so-called 'free' flight."

Dale has serious skepticism issues. I try to give the Visa folks the benefit of the doubt, preferring to believe the best about people. I am optimistic in that way. Dale, on the other hand, has been known to shred mail without even opening it, even if the envelope very clearly states, *"You can't afford to miss out on this offer! Respond at once, or you will contract scurvy!"* Like I want to risk contracting the same disease that plagued the crew of the *Santa Maria*?

Dale and I have very different approaches to spending, but I don't allow this to be the source of conflict in our home. On the contrary, the conflict usually happens outside our home when we are on vacation and I decide to make an impulse purchase with a credit card.

We were close to 200 miles from home during one vacation when we happened upon a "specialty item" store that had a small stock of solar-paneled, fan-cooled pith helmets at an incredibly reasonable price. I tried one on, and it was awesome. I mean, a regular British-style pith helmet would have been great, but this model had a small fan built right into the top of it. All I needed to do was step into the sunlight, and the solar panel converted the energy into a cooling breeze. It was a truly exceptional find, and I had never seen a helmet like this anywhere else.

"I'm going to get one," I told Dale.

She looked at the price tag. "Fifty dollars?" she gasped. "What in the world are you thinking?"

"Not to worry, my sweet," I replied. "I just happen to have a credit card on me."

"Which makes it free?" she asked, arms folded.

"Basically," I said. "They don't charge us interest for thirty days, so it is like getting a free loan. Besides, if things get a little tight, I can just stretch out the payments."

"You're right!" she exclaimed. "You could just add this charge to the tacky Sumo wrestler doll you bought across the street a few minutes ago, and all the other weird toys you have been buying with reckless abandon. You could just pay the minimum on all your credit cards and stretch out the payments forever!"

"That's the spirit!" I replied. "With any luck, I'll be dead before they are paid off."

"Dave, the credit card companies absolutely love people like you," Dale stated.

I blushed at the compliment. "I suppose that's why they keep sending me all those nice offers."

She made me put the helmet back on the rack and threatened to eliminate ten of my credit cards if I tried to make any more unbudgeted purchases.

Dale likes to mull over her spending decisions, sometimes for years. I mulled once for about five minutes, but I didn't like it, so I stopped. It isn't like I horribly overspend or don't pay my bills. I do pay them. I just don't monitor them as closely as Dale. She thinks we should track all of our bills monthly and know precisely how much we owe. She also thinks it is a good idea to balance the checkbook, which I think is the most boring task imaginable. "We still have checks, so what's the worry?" is my financial motto.

When it comes to fiscal matters, I am waaaaaay more flexible than Dale. But because I want to be happily married—as opposed to hospitalized—finances are an area in which I have had to do some changing in order to adapt to her comfort level.

For instance, I have learned that my impulse spending can ruin a vacation for her. If there is ever a time when I am tempted to go into spending mode, it's when we are on vacation. But many activities or purchases that I consider fun, she considers wasteful and even stupid. (The people who make wind-up, chattering teeth will *never* make a sale to Dale. I, on the other hand, have purchased several pairs over the years. One never knows when one will need a backup pair, perhaps as an emergency wedding gift.)

Dale can't really relax and have fun on a vacation unless she incorporates a least a measure of frugality into the planning and execution of the trip. So if we are driving to our destination, she will often pack food. My tendency is to simply pull into a burger joint along the way and buy food whenever we are hungry. But I have gotten used to the fact that we are going to have cheese and crackers, salami, apple slices, carrots, trail mix, and that kind of stuff in the car on a long trip. If we do that, then Dale can enjoy eating out periodically without worrying about how much we are spending. And I have come to grips with the fact that we are also going to take some extra time to look for package deals, special prices on accommodations, and discounts on activities.

Frankly, Dale's approach has saved us a *lot* of money over the years, and I have to admit that I have not suffered many ill effects from missing out on all those opportunities to visit fast-food joints off the freeway, even though Dale makes me include roughage in my diet.

But while I have learned to moderate my purchasing habits for Dale's sake, she has likewise moved in my direction. I do *not* like to shop. I do not like to agonize and dither and hesitate over a mere purchase. I like to walk in, find what I like, buy it, and leave in just about as much time as it took you to read this sentence. I consider shopping a necessary evil, an unfortunate requirement, a baneful responsibility. She thinks it is a delightful challenge, a competitive sport, a jolly romp. So we both have had to budge to avoid driving each other crazy.

Sometimes my "strike-while-the-iron-is-hot" viewpoint is a better approach than Dale's "let's-think-this-over-for-a-few-decades" approach. This was nowhere more apparent than when we were trying to purchase a house in the middle of a hot real-estate market in the summer of 2002. Houses were selling within days of being listed—and sometimes within hours. It was pure insanity. There was even one instance where a guy was talking with his wife over breakfast, and he casually asked, "What do you think about putting our house on the market?" Suddenly, four real-estate agents leaped through the window, wrestled him to the floor, and gave him noogies until he agreed to sign a contract.

Dale and I had been looking at houses for weeks, but other buyers were always beating us to the finish line. We had to reorient our lives completely during those weeks so that the split second our agent phoned us, we could drop whatever we were doing and race to another newly listed home before the rest of the mooing stampede of buyers arrived.

One day our agent called about yet another home, and even though the timing was not terribly convenient, I leaped out of the chair and told the dentist he could finish the filling later.

We walked into the house. I looked around the living room for precisely five seconds (I am not exaggerating) and told the agent, "We'll take it."

"Can we at least see all the rooms?" Dale asked.

We wasted five entire minutes poking around the place,

and then Dale agreed that we should make an offer. But, alas, we were too late. Someone had already made an offer that was accepted even though our offer would have been higher.

I made a backup offer, but the listing agent told us not to get our hopes up. "The first offer is very solid, so I would advise you to keep looking," she said. "You need to mentally let this one go."

Deflated, Dale and I decided to reconsider the whole idea of buying a home. The market was too intense. We went home and started planning possible modifications to our existing house.

A week later, I was 500 miles away on a business trip when my cell phone chirped. It was the realtor. "Mr. Meurer, the house you wanted is available," she said. "The other escrow fell through. You are the first person on my list to call, but I have several others. If you want the house, I need to know immediately."

I asked her to give me ten minutes so I could call Dale. I was elated as I punched in our home number, but by the time the phone rang I had a sinking feeling in my chest. Dale and I had pretty much decided against buying a house, and we had mentally shifted gears into the "let's-just-add-a-room" mode. I was used to making quick decisions, but I was pretty sure that Dale would not be willing to make a huge financial commitment under a five-minute deadline. She would probably want to see the house again, talk it over, run the numbers, ask advice—all reasonable desires, but impossible under the circumstances.

She answered the phone.

"Hi, Hon," I said. "The house is for sale again. The agent just called. But she has a bunch of other interested parties, so you literally have to decide right now if you want it. I hate to spring this on you, but that's the scoop. What do you want to do?"

I braced for what I knew would be the answer. She didn't want to rush into a decision like this, and we had already come to grips with staying in our current home, especially since we had fixed it up to sell so it was in better shape than ever, we had so much history in it, the yard was perfect for having friends out on the deck, and it was cheaper to just stay where we were. ...

"Let's take it," she said.

"What did you just say?" I asked, blinking.

"Tell her yes," Dale answered.

"Dale, did you just make an instant decision about a financial matter?" I asked.

"I learned it from you," she said.

So we bought the house.

As with so many other areas of life, we have changed each other when it comes to making financial decisions. We have learned from each other's perspectives, benefited from each other's strengths, and adapted to each other's desires.

Because of Dale, I am less rash than I would otherwise be. And because of me, Dale has become less guilt-ridden about spending a few bucks. This combination has worked out pretty well. However, with all the money we saved, you'd think she could cut me some slack on the solar-powered pith helmet.

She did ultimately strike a deal with me. "Dave, in the event you ever take a trip to Egypt without me, you can buy the ugly helmet."

I think I got the bad end of that bargain.

Fireproofing
Your Life

CHAPTER THIRTY-TWO

In one of the more interesting ironies of my youth, the local volunteer fire department was a main supplier of Fourth of July fireworks. Selling these extremely flammable objects generated significant annual revenue for the department, and the fireworks also ensured that the volunteers had numerous opportunities to put their training to good use. So it was a win-win situation for everyone.

The fireworks manufacturer labeled the fireworks "safe and sane," but that phrase assumed that 1) children would not be using the flammable materials without adult supervision, and 2) children would not modify the fireworks in such a manner as to render them extremely dangerous.

Both of those assumptions proved to be grossly optimistic.

As a ten-year-old, I routinely visited the fireworks stand and had the following conversation:

ME: "I would like one Blaster Fountain, a package of gold sparklers, three pinwheels, and a 'Piccolo Pete,' please."

VOLUNTEER FIRE DEPARTMENT GUY: "Is your mom or dad with you?"

ME: "No, but I'm sure they won't mind."

VOLUNTEER FIRE DEPARTMENT GUY: "Well, I guess it's all right, then. Do you need matches?"

ME: "Lots. Thank you."

Having performed this transaction and obtained my supplies, I would head home and tape my "Piccolo Pete" (a flaming, whistling flare) to a toy car, creating what amounted to a small and unsteerable missile on wheels. Part of the thrill was chasing the careening, flame-spewing invention in whatever random direction it launched itself. Fortunately, I always managed to put out the small fires that I inadvertently started.

Looking back, I shudder when I think of all the havoc I could have wreaked upon my neighborhood. It would have been bad enough if my close calls had been restricted to the Fourth of July, but, alas, fire was waaaaaay too interesting to leave alone for more than five or ten minutes.

I still recall the day a neighbor kid and I decided to get rid of a tree stump in his backyard. We tried whacking it with an axe for awhile, but progress was slow and boring, so we decided that burning it was the preferred method of removal. And what better way to burn an unsightly stump than to douse it with a generous slosh of gasoline?

We figured we could have the thing reduced to ashes before my friend's mom got back from the store, a trip she never took without first launching into an emphatic and almost shrill lecture to the effect that we *had better not do anything stupid this time,* and if we thought for *one second* that we were too old for a *spanking* we had another thing coming, and we better not even *think* about touching a lighter.

We promised. And we managed to not touch a lighter, even though we were sorely tempted. Instead, we flicked a match at the gas-soaked stump and watched in stunned horror as a roaring ball of flame shot skyward, licking the branches of an overhanging tree and setting fire to dozens of dry maple leaves. Flaming debris rained down all over the yard, fire from heaven pouring down upon the sons of disobedience. We scampered from spot fire to spot fire, stomping and yelling and acting like the young idiots we were. We managed to limit the damage pretty well, except for one piece of lawn furniture that had seen better days anyway—not that this argument was remotely persuasive to our parents. With all the yelling and punishments, you'd think we had robbed a bank or something.

I firmly believe that a guardian angel was watching over us, and I also suspect that he was eventually retired due to a nervous condition.

Many years later, as an adult, I was on a work-related tour of a national forest in the aftermath of a devastating wildfire. The area was a blackened moonscape, with all of the formerly green things now black or gray. A firefighter pointed out that many of the standing charred trees were lopped off at mid-height. "This fire was so hot that it created its own weather," he said. "It was kind of like a tornado in here. The wind was so strong it was snapping trees in half."

Try to imagine an inferno so powerful that it can break a mature tree as easily as you can snap a pencil. Let your mind replay the coverage you saw of the horrific fires that consumed Southern California in October 2003. Ponder the unstoppable walls of fire that overwhelmed the best efforts of an army of firefighters. And contemplate the fact that such a raging, destructive beast can be unleashed with a tongue of flame no larger than the one that flickers softly on the dinner table at your favorite romantic restaurant.

"Likewise," we read in James 3:5–6, "the tongue is a small part of the body, but it makes great boasts. Consider what a great forest is set on fire by a small spark. The tongue also is a fire, a world of evil among the parts of the body. It corrupts the whole person, sets the whole course of his life on fire, and is itself set on fire by hell."

These are incredibly strong words, but mull them over for a moment. How many husbands, wives, and children have been emotionally scorched by flaming invectives of uncontrolled tongues? How many hearts have been scalded? How many relational bridges have been burned?

The pain inflicted by the tongue can be every bit as real and brutal as the pain caused by a punch to the kidneys. There is no excuse—none, never—for causing that kind of pain. There is never an excuse for angry outbursts. For hurtful words. For caustic words. For sarcastic words.

An apology, no matter how deep and sincere, cannot retract hurtful words that may haunt someone for years. As helpful and important as an apology can be, it is so much better not to engage in an action that requires an apology.

I admitted in an earlier chapter that one of my weaknesses is anger. When I am angry, I am capable of saying stupid and hurtful things. I therefore need to be very cognizant of this flaw and work hard at overcoming it. By God's grace and with Dale's help, I have made progress. But I still have a long way to go. If I indulge my flaw, I can start an emotional inferno. So can you.

One wimpy, dishonest way people try to avoid responsibility for their words is to say something bad and then say, "I didn't mean it."

If they didn't mean it, they wouldn't have said it. Our tongues do not operate independently of our wills or our minds. We speak exactly what is on our minds and in our hearts. "For out of the overflow of the heart the mouth speaks," Jesus said (Matthew 12:34).

Kids can be corrected with firmness, but loving firmness. If you need to talk out something difficult with your spouse, do it openly but not hurtfully. Watch your words. Don't start an emotional conflagration.

One way to get our tongues under control is to fill our hearts and minds with God's Word—God's thoughts, God's viewpoint. Our tongues simply reveal what's inside us, so our mouths are not the real issue. The core of the matter is our hearts. Let's ask God daily to help us change, to help us speak healing and encouraging words, and to help us as we seek to conform to His moral image. He is always pleased to answer *this* prayer. I suggest praying it daily.

It's Your Serve

CHAPTER THIRTY-THREE

Now that you have made your way through most of this book, gleaning quite a bit of information about what kind of a guy I am, what I value, and what makes me tick, you are in a position to be properly horrified to discover that my church leaders allow me to participate in lay ministry. I realize that you may be tempted to ask, "What kind of lunatics are these people? Have they no standards at all?" But before you rush to judge them, realize that they did not have much choice.

The Bible is replete with directives urging all of us to play a role in ministry. The apostle Paul, for example, went out of his way to note that each one of us has a place to serve (see 1 Corinthians 12:1–30).

Slice it and dice it any which way you like, but the phrase "each one" includes me. And if it can encompass someone as immature as me, it surely includes you. (Fortunately, it also includes my wife. So much of my potential to mess things up is counterbalanced by Dale's ability to fix things. After living with me for more than two decades, she has so much experience in damage control that she is regularly consulted by FEMA.)

The Bible makes the sweeping assertion that all of us are called to serve and divinely equipped to serve. Whether or not we feel adequate for the task is wholly irrelevant. Feeling inadequate is not a ticket out of service. Nor is feeling busy. Not all of us can do high-profile things, but we can do *something*.

So, offer to do something, if you aren't already. For instance, I once offered to do an exposition of the book of Titus through the medium of interpretive dance. The pastor checked the church schedule and found that every Sunday was booked for the next fifty-seven years, but at least I offered. (Dale subsequently volunteered us to teach fifth-grade Sunday school, and the children's pastor said we could as long as Dale ensured that I would act at least as mature as the kids.)

Proverbs 11:25 captures an interesting life principle of giving something back: "He who waters will himself be watered" (NASB). This principle applies to you and me as individuals, but I think it also applies to our marriages. As we pour ourselves out in serving others, God will fill us back up. We can be "watered" by the mysterious process whereby the Holy Spirit empowers us even as we feel spent. We can also be "watered" by the very people we are serving.

So far, this book has largely emphasized your relationship with your spouse—what you do for each other. I have urged you to carve out time for each other, to maintain your relationship, to guard against overcommitment, and to cut back on external activities where necessary. So this call to service may sound as if I am reversing course, but I'm really not.

Indeed, if you have been taking care of each other, if you

have been strengthening your marriage, if you have been building a strong home life, you are probably in an excellent position to give something back. Even if it feels like a stretch, even if you feel too busy, you and your spouse need to be involved in service.

In our case, Dale and I are involved in a new ministry called "Impact Groups." These small groups are formed to address all kinds of needs in the church family. Our group is called "Family Matters," and its purpose is to strengthen marriages and family relationships.

To be very frank, the invitation to help lead this group came at an awful time in our lives. We felt maxed out with other things going on. We felt stretched too thin. We felt unprepared. But we did it anyway, and an interesting thing happened. We seem to be receiving more than we give. Even as we give to other couples, they are giving back to us—empathizing with our struggles, praying for our dilemmas, encouraging us in our walks with God. "He who waters will himself be watered." This is a God thing. In giving, we receive.

Although all of us married couples need to tend and nurture our own relationships, we cannot focus exclusively on that relationship. We all need rich, nurturing interaction with other people as well.

Indeed, much of the richest and deepest ministry is not going to come from the church staff. Ideally, the pastors and staff are equipping us to perform the innumerable good works God has called us to complete. Writing out a check is not enough. God calls us to give of ourselves.

As we give back, as we serve others, we discover the real meaning in life. If I find myself going for a long period of time without being meaningfully involved in the lives of others, it starts to feel as if life is about car repairs, paying bills, grocery shopping, tax returns, mowing the grass, washing the car, and all the other zillions of necessary but ultimately transitory activities.

I do not want to leave this life with a bunch of people standing around my gravesite saying, "Well, he didn't do much for anyone, but at least he regularly had his car lubed."

There is a satisfaction, a sense of fulfillment, that only comes from being involved in the lives of others. It can be messy, time-consuming, even painful work. But it is eternal. It is the work of God performed through us. The amazing thing is that He insists on forming a partnership with people like, um, me.

Your marching orders? Get involved. You two can make a great team for God's kingdom.

In Case You Hadn't Noticed, You're Not Twenty Anymore

CHAPTER THIRTY-FOUR

Climbing the sheer vertical wall named El Capitan in Yosemite National Park is an amazing, grueling, dangerous, exhilarating, and utterly exhausting ordeal. Anyone who manages that laborious feat will never forget it.

Our family drove to Yosemite in the summer of 2002, and I spared no expense to outfit us with everything we would need for our outdoor adventure. "Please pass the Cheetos," I said to Dale as we sat comfortably in our lawn chairs watching distant, tiny figures slowly scaling the towering granite slab of El Capitan. In addition to lawn chairs, we also had comfy pillows, binoculars, and cookies.

I will never be one of those people who cherish the memory of conquering El Capitan. I admired it from a distance, but I never even touched it, much less dangled from it. The most reckless thing I have ever dangled is a participle in Mrs. Wilson's seventh-grade English class, and the most dire consequence was losing five points off my essay (which was a fairly modest consequence when you compare it to the prospect of death on the rocks).

Instead of scaling El Capitan, we took the hiker-friendly "Mist Trail" up to Nevada Falls. At night, we slept in a tent cabin that featured beds, blankets, and a wood-burning stove so we wouldn't be chilly. I really did have to rough it one day when I had to wait an entire ten minutes to be seated at a park restaurant. But other than that traumatic hardship, our trip was all great.

I am okay with the fact that I will never do many daring things. I won't climb Everest, command a team of sled dogs, or race a car in the Indy 500. I won't be an Olympic diver unless the criteria are modified to award high marks for "biggest splash" and "most frantic arm-waving after being pushed from platform."

I am a middle-aged guy who has a desk job and enjoys taking walks with his wife. I don't run marathons. I don't run at all unless there is an emergency requiring swift movement, such as my house being threatened by a meteorite or a Tupperware party.

There comes a point in life, usually in middle age, where we either come to grips with reality or become panicked idiots who do stupid things. Some people my age suddenly get seized with the realization that by choosing A, they did not choose B. But they suddenly *want* B and C and D. They want it all. Simple logic says they can't have it all, but they are not thinking logically. So they dump their spouses. Drop the kids. Get replacements. Buy a sleek car. Try a new career. Get a new "look." Fill in the blank. They lunge from change to change, trying to grab all the gusto they can before they croak, just like the beer commercial advised.

When I say we need to come to grips with reality, I do

not mean we have to settle into a rut, stay in a boring job, or give up on our dreams. Indeed, I went back to school later in life and made a huge career change. I was forty when I inflicted my first book on the unsuspecting public. I was in my mid-forties when I finally tried okra (an experience from which I am still recovering). I am currently planning a trip to an exotic destination that was featured in one of the Indiana Jones movies, but I don't plan to leap off a horse or get dragged by a German tank. I don't even plan to get sunburned.

Coming to grips with reality means coming to grips with the fact that you and I cannot turn back the clock and make choices that were once open to us but are now closed.

Twenty-five years ago I could have joined the army and, if I was good enough, I could have become an elite Ranger and jumped out of airplanes on covert, perilous missions in foreign lands. That is no longer a live option. The army does not enlist people my age, and they certainly would not send someone in my physical condition on a mission against a trained, fit enemy force unless the goal of the mission was to cause the enemy to double up in bellyaches of mirth. Therefore I will never have an army career.

I have a good friend named Chuck Holton, who is a former Army Ranger. If you are not familiar with that segment of the armed forces, to be a Ranger means that you are part of a very small, elite group of warriors. Rangers are the tip of the spear, so to speak. So Chuck went through extraordinary training, was armed to the teeth, leaped from planes, landed at night on enemy soil, shot at enemy soldiers, ran through whizzing bullets, threw grenades, and did all the stuff you imagine when you think of an Army Ranger. (If you want an outstanding insight into what Ranger life is like, as well as some really great spiritual lessons drawn from the life of a warrior, pick up Chuck's excellent book, *A More Elite Soldier*.)

But Chuck left that life, got married, had kids, and today lives on a farm. By choosing civilian life, he gave up the right to do some of the gutsy things he used to do. If he started tossing grenades at the gophers on his farm, the local sheriff would probably have some harsh words for him—or worse.

When he chose not to make the army a career, Chuck by definition gave up one thing in favor of something else. He still does risky and semi-insane things, such as rappelling from cliffs and—more dangerous yet—taking teen youth groups on multinight camping trips. But these activities do not typically involve grave peril unless the teenagers do the cooking.

Two dozen years ago, the number of potential marriage partners available to me numbered in the millions. Technically, I could have asked any single woman in the world to marry me. But once I married Dale, all of those other options vanished. (And I am keeping her, so there. It isn't my fault that you other guys missed your big chance to marry the sweetest woman on the planet.)

Coming to grips with reality means that I differentiate between the options that are open and the options that are off-limits. It means I realistically assess my life and try to choose wisely.

The psalmist prayed, "Teach us to number our days aright, that we may gain a heart of wisdom" (Psalm 90:12). Wise men and women take stock of their lives and react not with panic but with planning. In contrast, fools look at their remaining days, panic because time is short, and decide to gorge themselves on all their desires, whether they are good or evil.

Of all of the many choices I have made during the course

of my life, quite a few were on the mark, and I would make them again. Some were stupid, and I wish I could take them back. Since I can't be twenty again, the following questions are relevant: "What do I do with the days left to me?" "What is the best way to use my time and talent?" "How do I best love and serve the woman I made those vows to?" "How can I lead a fulfilling, God-honoring life from this point forward?"

In my case, coming to grips with reality includes the acceptance of a certain level of regret for paths I did not take, words I should not have spoken, opportunities I missed, and friendships I failed to deepen. I also made some poor financial decisions that will take a lot of time to tidy up. I did not do some things for and with my kids when they were younger, and now the opportunity is gone. I had a chance to say the right words at the right times, but I choked sometimes.

I never learned to play the piano, and I really wish I had. Although nothing prevents me from taking it up now, I know myself well enough to know that I do not have the patience to learn how to play, and I am also otherwise occupied with a different keyboard—one with letters on it. I also know myself well enough to know that I won't learn to snowboard, even though my son Brad clearly has a blast doing that sport. If I were twenty years younger … but I am not.

I do have a goal of getting in better physical shape, but I am never going to pass for an athlete. I may pass for an accountant. Currently I am not capable of climbing El Capitan, and I am unwilling to make the enormous effort it would take to get into good enough shape to pull it off. That's reality.

There are so many ways in which my life has not unfolded as I thought it would or as I had hoped it would. I am guessing that I am by no means unusual in this regard.

We all have regrets. None of us is exactly who we wish we were. Something in us longs for perfection, but we can't have it in this life. None of our experiences will be perfect. We won't have the perfect marriage, or family, or career, or friends, or … anything.

The closest we each get to a "do-over" is the day we repent of our messed-up pasts and ask God for a fresh start in life. We can't go back, but by the grace of God we can go forward. We can enjoy the life we have now. We can enjoy who we are now. We do not have to rue the past or mourn over lost chances. And we can enjoy looking at a mountain we cannot climb.

When we are tempted to panic, we need to remember that someday we will, in fact, have it all. If we have been adopted into God's family, He has made us "co-heirs with Christ" (Romans 8:17). I don't know exactly what that means, but I understand enough to know that it is huge. If I am sharing in the inheritance of Christ Himself, I am inheriting something of staggering proportions.

Quoting in part from Isaiah, the apostle Paul wrote, "No eye has seen, no ear has heard, no mind has conceived what God has prepared for those who love him" (1 Corinthians 2:9). I have a hunch that in the new creation, we can climb any mountain we wish. We will be immortal, dazzling, powerful beings.

The beer commercial only told half the story. We only go around once in this life, but there is a bigger and bolder life to come. The wise man lives and plans and chooses in light of the life to come.

Don't panic. Plan.

Do You Hear What I Hear?

CHAPTER THIRTY-FIVE

I was settling into my airline seat as the flight attendant began his list of obligatory preflight announcements, which most seasoned travelers ignored. After all, they had heard it a hundred times.

"If you need to get into the overhead compartment during the flight, you will find that you don't fit," he said.

I looked up at him and smiled. Ninety-seven percent of the other passengers appeared to have missed it.

"Please note that the captain has turned on the no-smoking sign, so there will be no smoking for the duration of your life." His eyes were twinkling as he continued. "Please do not congregate by the forward lavatory or near the cockpit. If you rush toward the cockpit during the flight, the rest of us reserve the right to beat you to death."

The guy was a riot, and most people didn't even hear him. Or, more accurately, they tuned him out. They heard him without hearing him. Sooner or later, most of us have a similar experience with our spouses.

Consider this example:

WIFE (from kitchen): "Honey, I just finished all the little dessert tarts for the Paulsons' baby shower. I made exactly enough for the invited guests, so please don't touch them. I've been slaving over this stove all day, so I'm going to hop in the shower really quick, and then I have to run. You can have the leftovers in the fridge. Okay?"

HUSBAND (with face in newspaper): "Okay."

WIFE: "If Janet calls, tell her I'll be a little late picking her up, but I'll be there. These tarts were just so time-consuming. I'm running a bit behind. Got that?"

HUSBAND: "Okay."

Thirty minutes later ...

HUSBAND: "Hey, Janet called for you. Sounded worried. She asked if you were already at the shower, and I heard the water running so I told her yes. You might want to call her back right away. I think she's having a bad day. By the way, those little fruit things you made were great. I had so many I think I ruined my dinner."

It is because of these little communication lapses that most states have enacted laws banning homicide.

Sooner or later, each of us is guilty of zoning out and utterly ignoring our spouses. We would never have done this while we were dating unless we planned a life of celibacy. But as time goes on, we can slip into behavior that would get us fired if we did it on the job. Consider this scenario:

BOSS: "I need you to drop the Worthington project and get the Finkleman file ready for the audit. They need it a week earlier than we thought. It has to be on my desk on

Monday morning by ten o'clock. And tell everyone to post-pone the Maui Madness Party until we plow through this project. Got it?"

Monday morning …

YOU: "Good morning, boss. Mr. Finkleman stopped by awhile ago, but I told him he was off by a week. He looked very upset. Probably feels like a fool for driving all the way down here on the wrong day. I told him he could join us for the luau on the fourth floor, but he must not be into ethnic food. He actually tore off my lei and fed it into the shredder."

None of us would dream of tuning out our bosses like this, so what makes us think we can tune out our spouses?

Listening is a way of letting someone know that he or she matters. When our spouses are speaking to us, we need to go out of our way to make eye contact and really listen. To do anything less is simply rude. James 1:19 instructs us to be "quick to listen, slow to speak."

When we actively, attentively, and conscientiously listen, we not only ensure that we really hear our spouses, but we communicate something that cannot be communicated by our words. Listening shows a deference and honor to our spouses. We did it when we were young and in love, and we need to do it when we are old and in love.

I say this as someone who can be quite guilty of tuning out other people, including Dale. I am barraged with so much "input" that I can lapse into zombie mode.

I cannot listen while I am reading.

I cannot listen while I am typing.

I cannot listen while I am staring at the TV.

I cannot listen while I am daydreaming about an unre-lated topic.

Jesus was fond of saying, "He who has ears to hear, let him hear." It's good advice. Are we listening?

(Important last piece of marital advice to guys: If you eat more than six of those little fruit tarts in a single sitting, it can really give you an upset stomach. A few Tums will help a lot.)

Readers' Guide

For Personal Reflection or Group Discussion

Readers' Guide

I know, I know. It seems kind of weird to have a discussion guide in what is largely a humor book. But give it a try. Part of good spousekeeping involves engaging in open and honest discussion, sharing views, and comparing perspectives. If you and your spouse will each read a chapter and then share your responses to the questions, you can spark important and even serious discussions.

I hope you will understand each other better through the pages of this book. I think you will, because many of the issues raised are common to most marriages. I also hope you will laugh a lot together as you read. But I'd like you to go deeper than that. C'mon, try the discussion questions. They won't hurt—much. Or if they do hurt, it will be a good kind of hurt.

God bless your marriage.

—Dave Meurer

CHAPTER 1

1. Yes, research proves that every day women use about twice as many words as men do. Plus, women often find talking to be a prelude to passion. In light of this, would you agree that God deliberately forces guys into a position in which they must learn to talk more? Why or why not?

2. Beyond the obvious physical differences, which key differences between you and your spouse keep rising to the forefront?

3. What steps have you taken, or do you need to take, to accommodate these differences more effectively?

4. In Matthew 19:4–6, we read, "'Haven't you read,' he [Jesus] replied, 'that at the beginning the Creator "made them male and female," and said, "For this reason a man will leave his father and mother and be united to his wife, and the two will become one flesh"? So they are no longer two, but one. Therefore what God has joined together, let man not separate.'" Here, Jesus strongly affirmed that the idea of marriage originated with God and is not a mere convention invented by humans. How does Jesus' statement influence your view of your marriage?

CHAPTER 2

1. Does your spouse have a God-given right to insist that you get an annual physical checkup? Why or why not?

2. In your opinion, which is worse: a prostate exam or a mammogram? (Hint: The author votes for the one that starts with P.)

3. "The wife's body does not belong to her alone but also to her husband. In the same way, the husband's body does not belong to him alone but also to his wife" (1 Corinthians 7:4). What are the implications of this passage? How does this passage relate to the "one-flesh" principle Jesus affirmed?

4. Paul wrote, "Submit to one another out of reverence for Christ" (Ephesians 5:21). What do you think this passage means in the context of marriage? How would you restate it in your own words? What are some practical ways in which this directive can be applied?

CHAPTER 3

1. "I feel so much better now that I've given up hope." *What kind of comment is that?* you may be thinking. What I want to say is that we

need to accept the reality that raising kids well is really hard work. Accepting the reality of the hardship really makes the job easier. People who won't accept reality end up on drugs, become workaholics, or do anything they can to avoid recognizing that a) life is hard, and b) parenting is even harder. How have you "given up hope" in order to make your life easier? What was the result?

2. Both moms and dads supply important emotional, physical, and spiritual support to their children. In what ways are the parenting roles of you and your spouse similar, and in what ways do they differ?

3. Jesus said, "Let the little children come to me, and do not hinder them, for the kingdom of heaven belongs to such as these" (Matthew 19:14). Children are clearly important to God! In what ways can we hinder them from coming to Jesus? In what ways can we encourage them?

4. If you have kids, where are you on the "helping-or-hindering" scale? Are you reading Bible stories to your younger children? Do you have your older children plugged into a church youth group? (If your teens don't want to attend a youth group, make them go anyway. Often they don't want to go to school, either. So what? Do what is in their best interest. A good youth group is worth its weight in diamonds.)

CHAPTER 4

1. Read Hebrews 10:24: "Let us consider how we may spur one another on toward love and good deeds." How does this verse apply to a marital relationship?

2. There is a huge difference between *encouraging* someone to be his or her best and simply *complaining* about his or her faults. How can we "spur one another on" to good stuff in ways that motivate instead of discourage?

3. Sometimes we get into bad habits, such as nagging, complaining, or manipulating to get our way. List three loving, positive replacements for those poor habits.

CHAPTER 5

1. What is something at which your spouse excels?

2. Have you mentioned to your spouse that you admire his or her talent in that particular area? Why or why not?

CHAPTER 6

1. If you have children, how have they enriched your marriage? How have they made things difficult for you?

2. Since God says our kids are both gifts and responsibilities of trust, how should that affect your view of your children?

3. Children are high-risk. They are free to make choices, for good or ill, just like Adam and Eve were free to make choices. In what ways has parenting helped you to better understand the heart of our Father in heaven?

CHAPTER 7

1. Which objects or mementos has your spouse given you that are filled with memory and meaning for you? What makes each one special?

2. What are some of your best memories of times you have spent with your spouse? Talk about these with him or her.

CHAPTER 8

1. What are some of the key interests and pleasures that you and your spouse enjoy together?

2. What are some of your interests that your spouse does not share?

3. In what ways have you and your spouse worked to broaden areas of shared interest?

4. There is no way my wife will ever get me interested in craft projects, and I realize that she is unlikely to develop an interest in golf. We are both okay with this. How well do you and your spouse communicate about and agree on how much time you each devote to different areas of interest?

CHAPTER 9

1. When we are rational and objective, most of us believe that what God says about right and wrong, good and bad, is wise and true. So why do we still choose to sin?

2. In your life, have you noticed a pattern, a process that you go through, when you are being tempted to believe a lie and to take a bite of the appealing but dangerous cake called temptation?

3. How can you and your spouse better help each other to avoid sin?

4. What do you need to do on your own to avoid giving in to temptations that lead to sin?

CHAPTER 10

1. How has your spouse helped you to see a situation more clearly?

2. Have you ever reversed your course based on something only your spouse could see in you? Why or why not?

3. The Bible speaks a lot about people who have eyes but do not see. In a tense exchange with self-righteous religious leaders of His day, Jesus said, "If … you claim you can see, your guilt remains" (John 9:41). We all need our spiritual sight restored. Have you ever asked Jesus to remove your spiritual blindness so you can start seeing things with new spiritual eyes? If yes, what happened? If no, why not?

CHAPTER 11

1. Have you ever gone to a yard sale together? If so, what happened? If not, why not?

2. God says that we are "created in Christ Jesus to do good works" (Ephesians 2:10). If you and your spouse are not already doing "good works," what opportunities are available in your area? Are you willing to pray that God will help you find just the right ministry opportunity?

CHAPTER 12

1. When your family or a good friend experienced a traumatic medical emergency or other major event, how did that situation affect you? Did it pull people together or push them apart? Why?

2. In the middle of an especially tough time, we often ask, "Why?" There is no answer to this question, at least not this side of eternity. God never said life would be easy, and in fact Jesus warned us, "In this world you will have trouble." But He added, "But take heart! I have overcome the world" (John 16:33).

3. Dale and I think a big part of faith is simply trusting that God is good and loves us deeply, even when circumstances are awful and everything seems to be going wrong. What do you think? Why?

CHAPTER 13

1. In what ways have you been changed by your spouse? Discuss at least one of them with him or her.

2. How has your spouse helped to "stretch" you, not only in small things such as learning to appreciate cauliflower, but in the bigger issues, such as your spiritual life?

3. What kind of "adventure" would you like to have with your spouse? What will it take to make it happen?

CHAPTER 14

1. When is it okay to rent a convertible for a weekend just to get it out of your system?

2. Ephesians 4:32 reads, "Be kind and compassionate to one another, forgiving each other, just as in Christ God forgave you" (see also Colossians 3:12–13). Why is forgiveness to be such a big part of our relationships with God and with the people we love?

3. The Bible is clear that we need to both forgive and be forgiven because we are flawed people and we all blow it. But some people make repeated requests for "forgiveness" and demonstrate no positive change in behavior. How should we address that kind of scenario?

CHAPTER 15

"I have learned to be content whatever the circumstances. I know what it is to be in need, and I know what it is to have plenty. I have learned the secret of being content in any and every situation, whether well fed or hungry, whether living in plenty or in want. I can do everything through him who gives me strength" (Philippians 4:11–13).

1. What was your most messed-up vacation or recreational outing like? Can you laugh about any of it as you look back on it now? Why or why not?

2. What spiritual lessons or insights have you gained from experiencing situations that go haywire?

3. How can we develop more God-centered attitudes?

CHAPTER 16

1. Which habits would you like to overcome? Which habits would you like to nurture? List them.

2. How do you feel about letting your spouse help you?

3. When can you discuss issues related to your habits together?

CHAPTER 17

1. How do you differentiate between wholesome joking/humor and hurtful joking/humor?

2. How sensitive are you to not making jokes at your spouse's expense?

3. Why is so much humor created at other peoples' expense?

CHAPTER 18

1. What was your worst car ever, and why?

2. What was your best car ever, and why?

3. Why do we find ourselves wanting certain possessions in order to project certain images of ourselves?

4. How should the fact that our truest identity lies in being children of God influence our view of all the external stuff?

5. Why is it so important to keep this "identity perspective" in mind?

CHAPTER 19

1. Discuss with your spouse your best Christmas memory and your worst holiday nightmare.

2. God really used Dale to help me get over my unrealistic expectations of a "perfect" Christmas. When has the advice or insight of your spouse significantly changed your thinking about a problem or family issue? What happened as a result?

3. God allowed Mary and Joseph to endure a difficult set of circumstances. They had to travel a long distance during the end stages of Mary's pregnancy, they could not even rent a simple room for the delivery, and they lived under the rule of an occupying Roman force. God often uses hard circumstances to help us grow spiritually. What have you learned during a hard time that you probably would not have learned if everything had gone just fine?

CHAPTER 20

1. What kind of a view of sex did you receive while growing up?

2. How does your view of sex affect your marriage—positively, negatively, or both?

CHAPTER 21

1. In 2 Timothy 3:16-17, we read, "All Scripture is God-breathed and is useful for teaching, rebuking, correcting and training in righteousness, so that the man of God may be thoroughly equipped for every good work." On a scale of one to ten (with one being low), how would you rate your grasp of the Bible?

2. How much time and intellectual energy might you be willing to commit to a systematic study of the Scriptures? Why?

3. Which obstacles will you have to face in order to spend more time studying the Bible?

CHAPTER 22

1. Who worries the most in your marriage? In what ways does this worry affect your marriage—for good or for bad?

2. Since we parents cannot control all the twists and turns of life, how can we strike a balance between allowing our children to take appropriate risks and being overprotective and overly concerned?

3. What does it mean to you to entrust your family into God's care?

CHAPTER 23

1. Question for guys: Did your wife sit you down one day, look you in the eyes, and say, "Hon, I know you think it is romantic when you come home and hand me a single rose and give me a big hug and tell me I am the most important woman in the world to you. But what really sweeps me off my feet is when you come home and thumb through the mail and mutter about the bills, and then say what a lousy day you had and ask me what's for dinner. I can barely keep my hands off you when you do that." (If your wife answers "yes" to this question, then she is the only woman in the world to answer affirmatively.) Why is romance important to a marriage?

2. What can you do this week to surprise and delight your spouse and make him or her feel like you two are newlyweds again? (Note to women: For men, there is no real equivalent to flowers, with the possible exception of power tools. However, it is hard to arrange a tasteful

bouquet of drills and radial arm saws. But I have met few men who would not appreciate a head-to-toe body massage. Just a hint.)

CHAPTER 24

Ponder the following questions on your own rather than with your spouse.

1. If I am very honest with myself, not giving the "right" answer for someone else's consumption but answering what I really feel, on a scale of one to ten I would rate my satisfaction with my marriage as a ____. And here's why:

2. If you are not pleased with the score, which concrete, specific, practical steps can you take to improve your marriage? (Note: The question is not, "What can my spouse do to make me happier?" The question is, "What can *I* do to improve my marriage?")

3. If you start doing and thinking about things differently, how might your new attitudes and actions affect your mate's outlook—and possibly his or her actions?

CHAPTER 25

1. Do you and your spouse usually paddle in the same direction? Why or why not?

2. Which area(s) cause(s) the most significant disagreements in your marriage?

3. How might praying together about the issues that challenge you make a difference?

4. Knowing that God places a big premium on marital harmony, is there something—a desire, a dream, a plan—that you may need to reconsider because it is negatively affecting your marriage? If so, set aside some time soon when you can reevaluate it.

CHAPTER 26

1. What are the most troublesome weeds growing in your life?

2. Are you actively digging them up or ignoring them in the hope that they will go away? Why?

3. One reason God has given you your spouse is to help you cultivate good things in your life, while helping you yank out the weeds. Your spouse can be a tool in the hand of God. What will you do within the next week to encourage your spouse to help you cultivate the best things in your life?

CHAPTER 27

"Pride goes before destruction, a haughty spirit before a fall" (Proverbs 16:18).

"All of you, clothe yourselves with humility toward one another, because, 'God opposes the proud but gives grace to the humble'" (1 Peter 5:5).

1. In your own words, define the kind of "pride" that these verses warn against.

2. In the English language, the word *pride* is used in more than one way. Let's suppose a craftsman finishes a fine piece of furniture—a chair. He steps back to view the finished project and feels a deep sense of satisfaction in how it turned out. We say that he "takes pride in his work." That is, he dedicates himself to excellence and enjoys the sense of accomplishment. How does this form of pride differ from the "pride" God condemns?

3. A husband believed it was a sign of weakness to admit he was wrong or to apologize to his wife or his children. Even when he knew he was wrong, he would just ignore it. Why is this pattern of behavior so destructive in relationships?

4. An arrogant person is likely to ruin his or her relationships. Is your relationship with your spouse characterized by humility or pride? Explain your answer.

CHAPTER 28

1. What are some of the ways in which husbands and wives learn to take risks together?

2. If you were to face a big decision, such as changing careers and perhaps moving to a new city, how would you and your spouse reach a decision?

3. Is there something you have always dreamed of doing, yearned to do? Have you shared that dream with your spouse? If so, what happened? If not, why not?

4. Some people are naturally adventurous (risk takers), and some people value security and stability (risk averse). What is your tendency? What about your spouse? What are the benefits and drawbacks of each of these tendencies?

CHAPTER 29

1. What are you doing to regularly maintain your marriage? Be specific!

2. What in your marriage needs more attention?

3. A sticker on my windshield reminds me when my car needs an oil change. What little reminders can you use to remind you to recharge your marital battery?

4. When my car needs serious help, I hire a competent mechanic to diagnose and fix the problem. Sometimes a marriage is in such a dire state of neglect that the couple does not know how to repair the damage. If your marriage is stalled on the side of the road, are you willing to bring in some expert help? Why or why not? (I only go to mechanics who have been recommended by a qualified person. Likewise, I would not suggest simply picking a marriage counselor out of the phone book. Get a good recommendation first.)

CHAPTER 30

1. Because the spiritual battle we fight does not have explosions and bullets zipping over your head, do you find it easy to forget that the spiritual war is even going on? (Confession: I do.) What can you do to remind yourself about this war and to take this battle more seriously?

2. What specific things can you do to help protect yourself, your spouse, and your kids from the evil, spiritual arrows that are being shot at your marriage and home life?

CHAPTER 31

1. In what ways are finances a point of disagreement for you and your spouse? Why?

2. In your marriage, how do your spending and saving patterns differ from those of your spouse?

3. Have you ever, as a couple, taken a church-sponsored class in money management? If yes, how did it help you? If not, why not?

4. The Bible has more to say about money than just about any other subject. How committed are you and your spouse to discovering God's teachings about money?

CHAPTER 32

1. How well do you have your tongue under control? Are there some apologies you need to make for sharp words you've said?

2. Jesus said, "But I tell you that men will have to give account on the day of judgment for every careless word they have spoken. For by your words you will be acquitted, and by your words you will be condemned" (Matthew 12:36–37). What do you think of when you read this passage? What do you need to start doing differently?

3. The Bible says, "In your anger do not sin" (Ephesians 4:26). Anger is not inherently evil. Jesus became angry at injustice and hard-heartedness, yet He did not sin. How can a person express anger without sinning by word or by deed? What guidelines can you and your spouse use to help you during times of "heated" conversation?

CHAPTER 33

1. Which obstacles must you and your spouse overcome in order to serve other people?

2. When can you start serving others, if you aren't already? Tell one of your church leaders that you want to know how you can play a meaningful role in serving others. (Warning: That person may collapse. Have oxygen ready.)

3. If you already serve others, is it time to do more? Or perhaps to choose a different vehicle of service?

4. Discuss with your spouse a ministry you could perform together, if you aren't doing so already. Team-teach a children's Sunday school class, for example. Serve meals at a local mission. Drive a van for a church or parachurch ministry. Raise money for a crisis pregnancy center. Take meals to sick people. Lead a small-group Bible study. Do something for missionaries. Make sure that a soldier's family is doing okay while he or she is deployed abroad. The possibilities are endless.

CHAPTER 34

1.   Revelation 7:17 reads, "And God will wipe away every tear from their eyes." What does this verse mean to you?

2.   "If there is a natural body, there is also a spiritual body" (1 Corinthains 15:44). We are all wearing out physically (see James 4:14). Have you come to grips with that? Are you looking forward to the body to come, the life to come? Why or why not? What impact does this belief have on you? Why?

3.   What dream have you wanted to pursue but have not attempted? If it falls in the category of "open options"—that is, if it does not violate one of God's moral codes, cause you to break a promise, or do something unwise in relation to your spouse or your family—why not talk about it with your spouse? You may or may not decide to pursue it, but at least put it on the table and think it through. My wife and I jointly decided I should move out of a job in the grocery business to pursue a new career. We are glad about the decision. Again, coming to grips with reality does not mean you can't change, grow, or pursue a desire. It is about asking God for wisdom as you make your decisions.

CHAPTER 35

1.   Ever have one of those experiences when you had a complete conversation with your spouse but were just going through the motions, giving an occasional "uh-huh" while your mind was on something completely different and you pretty much missed everything your spouse said? (Welcome to the club.) What happened?

2.   Do you consider yourself an active listener? If not, what are some steps you can take to improve your listening skills?

3.   Ask your spouse if he or she feels like you really listen, and don't get all defensive if the answer is negative. (This is important stuff. Marriages are ruined over problems with communication, and failing to really listen can be a big part of the mess.) What, according to your spouse, can you do to improve in this area? (If you can restate in your own words what your spouse is telling you, and if your spouse agrees that you have captured the thought, you are listening well.)

The Word at Work Around the World

A vital part of Cook Communications Ministries is our international outreach, Cook Communications Ministries International (CCMI). Your purchase of this book, and of other books and Christian-growth products from Cook, enables CCMI to provide Bibles and Christian literature to people in more than 150 languages in 65 countries.

Cook Communications Ministries is a not-for-profit, self-supporting organization. Revenues from sales of our books, Bible curricula, and other church and home products not only fund our U.S. ministry, but also fund our CCMI ministry around the world. One hundred percent of donations to CCMI go to our international literature programs.

CCMI reaches out internationally in three ways:

- Our premier International Christian Publishing Institute (ICPI) trains leaders from nationally led publishing houses around the world.

- We provide literature for pastors, evangelists, and Christian workers in their national language.

- We reach people at risk—refugees, AIDS victims, street children, and famine victims—with God's Word.

Word Power, God's Power

Faith Kidz, RiverOak, Honor, Life Journey, Victor, NexGen — every time you purchase a book produced by Cook Communications Ministries, you not only meet a vital personal need in your life or in the life of someone you love, but you're also a part of ministering to José in Colombia, Humberto in Chile, Gousa in India, or Lidiane in Brazil. You help make it possible for a pastor in China, a child in Peru, or a mother in West Africa to enjoy a life-changing book. And because you helped, children and adults around the world are learning God's Word and walking in his ways.

Thank you for your partnership in helping to disciple the world. May God bless you with the power of his Word in your life.

For more information about our international ministries, visit www.ccmi.org.